Gay Bar

Gay Bar

The Fabulous, True Story
of a Daring Woman and Her Boys
in the 1950s

Will Fellows

and

Helen P. Branson

Introduction by

Blanche M. Baker, M.D.

The University of Wisconsin Press

The University of Wisconsin Press
1930 Monroe Street, 3rd Floor
Madison, Wisconsin 53711-2059
uwpress.wisc.edu

3 Henrietta Street
London WCE 8LU, England
eurospanbookstore.com

Gay Bar was first published in 1957 by Pan-Graphic Press, San Francisco,
copyright © 1957 by Helen P. Branson

Gay Bar: The Fabulous, True Story of a Daring Woman and Her Boys in the 1950s
by Will Fellows and Helen P. Branson
copyright © 2010 by the Board of Regents of the University of Wisconsin System

1   3   5   4   2

Printed in the United States of America

Library of Congress Cataloging-in-Publication Data
Fellows, Will.
Gay bar: the fabulous, true story of a daring woman and her boys in the 1950s /
Will Fellows and Helen P. Branson.
p.   cm.
Includes bibliographical references.
An expanded edition of the original 1957 publication "Gay Bar" by Helen P. Branson, interleaved with commentary and excerpts from letters and essays appearing in gay publications of the period.
ISBN 978-0-299-24850-5 (cloth: alk. paper)
ISBN 978-0-299-24853-6 (e-book)
1. Gay bars—California—Los Angeles.
2. Gay men—California—Los Angeles—Social conditions—20th century.
I. Branson, Helen P. Gay bar.   II. Title.
HQ76.3.U5F45   2010
306.76′627949409045—dc22
2010011528

To the Boys

In the millions who are silent and submerged, I see a potential, a reservoir of protest, a hope for a portion of mankind. And in my knowledge that our number is legion, I raise my head high and proclaim that we, the voiceless millions, are human beings, entitled to breathe the fresh air and enjoy, with all humanity, the pleasures of life and love on God's green earth.

Donald Webster Cory, *The Homosexual in America*

Preface

AMERICAN LIFE IN THE 1950s was vastly more complex and fascinating than popular imagination would suggest. Of particular interest to me, it was the period in which homosexuals emerged from the shadows, the crucible within which the modern gay rights movement originated. My chance discovery of Helen P. Branson's long out of print *Gay Bar* opened an illuminating window into those fretful, hopeful times.

Breakfasting in Saint Paul in 2006, my playwright friend Dean Gray and I discussed a script he was working on. The story centered on his Uncle Irvin, who grew up in the 1930s and 1940s on an Iowa farm and moved to Los Angeles in the 1950s in pursuit of a music career. Irvin killed himself there in 1963. Dean asked if I knew of any books or other materials that might provide insight into what it was like to be a gay man in Los Angeles in the 1950s.

About the only thing that came to mind was *Gay Bar*, a book that I had never seen but had noticed among the results of an online book search. Its snappy title and intriguing description had lodged in my mind. That same morning, Dean and I were delighted to find a copy of *Gay Bar* at Quatrefoil Library in Saint Paul. So began this foray into the long-gone Hollywood world of Helen Branson and her boys.

After Dean Gray's play, *Uncle*, had been staged in New York, Dean and I began to discuss creating a play based on *Gay Bar*. He would take the lead on playwriting, and I would try to find out more about Helen Branson. We knew from her book that Helen had been born in the mid-1890s, possibly in Nebraska, and that she had a grandson. I hoped to locate her grandson, though my chances for success seemed meager. I didn't know if he was still living, or if it was his mother or his father who was Helen's child.

Through the Social Security Administration, I obtained a copy of Helen's 1937 application. It indicated that she was born in Almena, Kansas, to Leo and Fannie Pyle, on December 17, 1896. At the time she filled out the form she was 40 years old, unemployed, living in Los Angeles. This was a compelling start, but what next? My friend Kim Karcher suggested that I do some research on Ancestry.com. To my astonishment I was soon looking at a 1930 U.S. Census form that detailed a household of three in Glendale, California: Helen P. Branson, 33, born in Kansas; Zebulon S. Branson, 35, born in Nebraska; and Helen C. Branson, 10, born in Idaho.

Zebulon! Also via Ancestry.com, Los Angeles County voter records from 1924 through 1948 gave biennial snapshots of the Branson family's home address and Helen's occupation. She went from a "housewife" in Glendale in 1924 to an "entertainer" in Hollywood in the late 1930s and early 1940s. About 1933 a separation occurred: Zebulon moved to Orange County, and Helen and her daughter stayed in West Hollywood. Helen's grandson still eluded me, but these were exciting discoveries. A picture of Helen's life in Los Angeles was beginning to emerge.

The online California Death Index revealed that Helen Pyle Branson died in Sacramento on January 7, 1977. Sacramento County supplied a copy of the death certificate, which confirmed that Helen had been divorced. Caroline B. Hammond of Sacramento was listed as the "informant" on the death certificate. I wondered who that person might have been— neighbor, friend, care provider?—but I did not pursue it. And then the crematorium provided the thrilling breakthrough, a copy of the cremation certificate on which Caroline B. Hammond was identified as "daughter." Of course! Helen C. Branson Hammond went by her middle name, Caroline, because her mother's name was Helen. Why hadn't I thought of that?

I was soon having lively conversations with Caroline, 88, and her son, Russell, 59. Both seemed stunned and delighted to have been discovered as Helen's descendents fifty years after her obscure little book was published. They were generous and candid in sharing their memories of the remarkable person they knew as Mother and Granny.

I concluded my quest to find living links to Helen Branson by trying to locate any gay man who had been acquainted with Helen or her bar. Success seemed unlikely. Helen used only pseudonyms in her book, for obvious reasons. Helen's daughter could not recall the names of any of her mother's gay pals, and none of the archival materials related to the book revealed their identities. Helen's bar was a tiny place in a very large and rapidly growing city with a highly transient population. More than fifty years later the youngest of Helen's boys would be about eighty years old and could be living far from Los Angeles. Posting my research notice in the senior services area of the L.A. Gay and Lesbian Center brought no response. My inquiries to Prime Timers chapters around the country brought several sketchy recollections of various L.A. gay bars, mostly in the 1960s and later, but nothing about Helen's.

Today one might regard Helen Branson as a woman ahead of her time, but for the homosexual men she befriended, she was there at just the right time. Reading Helen's observations on gay men's lives in the 1950s, I sometimes wondered what the men themselves would have said. I was thrilled to discover in two homophile periodicals, *ONE* magazine and *Mattachine Review*, a rich trove of contemporaneous commentary that amplified and complemented Helen's views. In voices authentic to the 1950s, gay men expressed their opinions, fears, pleasures, and hopes. And so the idea of this new edition of *Gay Bar* emerged, an interleaving of the book's original text with related writings from the same period, including a fuller portrait of Helen herself.

Gay Bar is a homespun memoir by a woman who enjoyed the company of homosexual men and deplored their plight. What the book lacked in literary quality, it more than made up for in audacity. Helen Branson's informal but earnest book appeared at a time when most books on "the homosexual problem" were written by male authorities, especially psychiatrists who viewed homosexuality as neurosis. Highlighting the buoyant and recently appropriated word "gay" was an edgy move, but *Gay Bar* was truly something new and startling. It was the first book by a heterosexual to examine the lives of homosexuals with admiration, respect, and love. And it was published under the author's real name at a time when homosexuality was anathema to most Americans, including many homosexuals themselves.

Gay Bar was also noteworthy as the first book published by Pan-Graphic Press in San Francisco. Co-owned by Mattachine Society members Harold Call and Donald Lucas, Pan-Graphic was itself a bold enterprise. It did printing for Mattachine and two other homophile groups, Daughters of Bilitis and ONE, Incorporated. That all three of these pioneering groups originated in California in the 1950s reflects the fact that, especially after World War II, Los Angeles and San Francisco were major destinations for American gays and lesbians in search of community, tolerance, and opportunity.

Helen Branson started writing *Gay Bar* in 1955, a year rife with witch hunts and other antihomosexual initiatives. It was only ten years after the end of Hitler's frenzy, in the midst of a growing civil rights movement, with many Americans intent on demonizing Communists and homosexuals. Moreover, many homosexuals themselves were inclined to see homosexuality as indeed a problem. A *Mattachine Review* writer described the threatening but not hopeless scenario: "So long as 'omniscient' psychiatry is a veritable Babel on what homosexuals are, public acceptance will be slow. Perhaps acceptance is not what awaits us. Psychiatrists may make good their aim to cure us all. Or they may decide variety is not without advantages.

"Two possible directions face us; one, a sort of 1984, a world of deadening conformity and regimentation, with psychiatrists for police, and the other, a more liberal, 'open' society, in which all would have latitude for working out their own destinies. And between these two chief possibilities, a number of middle roads open, offering greater or less freedom for social variants."

A thoroughgoing nonconformist herself, Helen wrote her little book in support of variety and freedom. To appreciate what *Gay Bar* represented when it appeared in 1957, it is essential to recognize that an enormously conformist conservatism pervaded American life at the time. *Mattachine Review* remarked in 1957 on "the creeping scourge of mediocrity that is becoming all too commonplace in our social structure today. Conformity—the tendency to avoid thought, discussion and action on unpopular subjects (the homosexual problem is only one of them)—is becoming a fashion. It hangs like a thread-suspended sabre over the heads of those who dare to speak out."

It is impossible now to comprehend the intensely conformist character of American culture in that time. But it is enlightening to consider that, in its current usage, the word "conformity" has pejorative connotations that did not exist until the counterculture of the 1960s and 1970s reshaped the American mindset. Until then, conformity was widely understood as a personal achievement in social adjustment, not as a failure in self-expression. To be like others was to do one's part in fostering social harmony and national strength.

In some ways this conformist imperative was as central to the sensibilities of homosexuals in the 1950s as it was of heterosexuals'. With gender roles part of the bedrock of conformity, blending in with the mainstream of regular Joes and Janes was tremendously important to many gay men and lesbians. Homophile organizations endorsed gender-role conformity as key to winning acceptance by "normals." But this chronic masquerading exacted a toll that was sometimes devastating. Homophile activist Bob Bishop of North Hollywood remarked on this in a letter to *Mattachine Review* in 1958: "In our culture, the spiritless homosexual is soon beaten down to the ground and forced to conform to a pattern for which he is completely unsuited. He soon learns to pass under the guise of masculinity and of course this role demands that he be critical of all overt homophile activity."

Gay Bar provides glimpses of an important and neglected aspect of gay American life in that era: Gays were often obsessed with conforming to mainstream gender norms themselves and demanding the same of others.

Helen Branson makes observations that pertain to this topic, as does Dr. Blanche Baker in the book's introduction. But this phenomenon is most richly documented in the words of gay men who were trying to navigate the hazardous cultural terrain of the 1950s.

This masculinity mania among homosexual men represented a huge change in American gay culture. In fact, the dominant mode of self-presentation among American gay men underwent a complete inversion from the first several decades of the 1900s to midcentury. An attitude of embracing, accentuating, even exaggerating one's femininity was replaced by an attitude of fleeing femininity and accentuating, even exaggerating, one's masculinity. Mr. B. of San Francisco described the feminine attitude in a letter to *ONE*: Homosexuals in the 1920s "all pretended to be more effeminate than we were to attract attention. Most people thought we were harmless, amusing clowns."

Donald Vining elaborated in the 1980s: "Many of today's gays . . . might well run into their closets and pull the door shut if they encountered a flock of their predecessors, who were often much gaudier and bawdier than most contemporary gays. Some of us did indeed avoid their flamboyant company, wince at their behavior, and try to merge indistinguishably with the run of humanity. Most, however, did not. We did not see ourselves as set apart from straights only by our sexual orientation. We conceived of ourselves as far superior beings—wittier, quicker to appreciate everything cultural, more sensitive, and if nature gave us the slightest assist, more stunning to look at." Gay people, Vining said, "didn't make themselves conspicuous to attract only the attention of their peers; they wanted straights to notice too—to notice and envy. They wanted society to notice and realize that this bright and beautiful being was one of those whom they derided as 'queer.'"

Psychotherapist Albert Ellis was obviously familiar with this pattern of gay self-appreciation. In a paper titled "How Homosexuals Can Combat Anti-Homosexualism" he advised that homosexuals should "abhor all feelings and actions which would tend to show others that they, the homosexuals, consider themselves in any way superior to . . . non-homosexuals." Ellis revealed his awareness of tight-knit gay communities when he said that gays should "avoid being over-clannish," should "resist in-group favoritism," should "refuse to help other homosexuals economically, socially, vocationally, or otherwise JUST because these others are inverts."

Ellis went on to advise that homosexuals "try to refrain from flaunting their homosexual tendencies in public, and should reserve their use of other-sex dress, mannerisms, vocal inflections, etc. to private gatherings." And whether in mixed company or among their own kind, Ellis believed that homosexuals "should avoid undue sentimentalism, super-romanticism, and self-pity and should accept the realities of everyday living. By the same token, they should avoid exaggerated cynicism and despair and grant reality its valid, if at times sombre, due."

Doc Ellis was just no fun at all. By the early 1950s, changes in American culture had made the gaudy, bawdy homosexual an endangered species. The reverencing of psychiatry, the disconcerting impact of Kinsey's sex research findings, the mindset of the postwar return to normalcy, the vilification of nonconformists and Communists—as a result of these and other influences, homosexuals were not likely to be regarded as harmless, amusing clowns.

Central to the demotion of the pansy was a broadening in the range of male types who identified as homosexual and chose to live accordingly. In the first several decades of the 1900s, men who were largely homosexual but not markedly effeminate were often quite likely to marry women and rear children, leading lives that were largely indistinguishable from those of normals. By midcentury these types of predominantly homosexual men who could have managed to pass quite convincingly as heterosexual were increasingly choosing not to do so. But effeminate self-presentation was not for them. Though living in ways that accommodated their homosexuality, it was important to them to accentuate and spotlight their masculinity.

This inversion of dominant self-concept among American homosexuals was a messy process. The clash of opposing sensibilities contributed to the severe "bitchery-butchery" that pervaded the 1950s homophile arena. "One of our headaches is the screaming, feminine-type homosexual," a Mattachine member told a reporter. "Most of us can't stand them and we have little luck persuading them to conform." A fellow who resigned from the Mattachine Society in 1954 offered a different view, lamenting that the organization was intent on excluding from membership not only Communists but also "the so-called 'swish.'" He remarked sarcastically that, compared to determining Communist Party connections, the identification of swishes was requiring more subtle approaches, "for only the holiest of holies have dared to judge where their behavior patterns end and the 'swish' begins."

Thus did the homophile world of the 1950s come to be dominated by masculinist values. By the early 1960s, homosexuals with more masculine self-presentation seemed to be stealing the spotlight from the pansies, perhaps even outnumbering them. "People still think in terms of the effeminate stereotype," said Donald Webster Cory, "but it is becoming widely known that this image represents only a small minority of the minority."

The lingering effects of the butch makeover driven by America's hyperconformist culture of the 1950s persist in the self-presentation of gay men today. Helen Branson and Blanche Baker would hardly disapprove, nor would Helen's boys. But they would all recognize it as a mask worn by uncommon men who from boyhood have special affinity with their mothers and grandmothers, sisters and girlfriends, gal pals and divas and golden girls. Helen's observations make it clear that she understood her own rapport with gay men to be rooted in this psychic resonance. By operating her bar during America's most antigay decade, Helen fostered safety, connection, and hope for her beloved boys. And because she chose to write a book in their behalf, we have this illuminating sketch of gay men's lives in a period of momentous challenge and change.

Will Fellows

Milwaukee, Wisconsin
February 2010

From the Dust Jacket
of the Original Edition

Casting a spotlight on one of those gathering places found in every large city . . . written by a woman who knows her subject from the inside out, GAY BAR tells the humor, the heartbreak, the piercing reality of the lives of people in and about a bar which caters to homosexuals.

But make no mistake about it. The people who are Helen Branson's customers are not the depraved and sinister characters so often presented as typical of the homosexual. Instead they are responsible, well-behaved human beings no different from anyone else except in the direction of their loves.

While GAY BAR is entertaining reading, its purpose is a serious examination of a pressing social problem. Few serious-minded persons will find it possible to disagree with the author's forthright advice when she says that if more parents understood their sons, then perhaps fewer homosexuals would find it necessary to seek companionship in the gay bars across the land. And if that happened, Helen is quick to admit, she wouldn't have so many customers!

Straight from the Shoulder . . .
"You won't find any statements in parentheses in my book," said Helen P. Branson as she turned in the final manuscript for publication. "I typed this

Helen Pyle Branson, Hollywood, 1957. Courtesy Caroline Branson Hammond and Russell Hammond.

myself on a Polish model typewriter. It had no parentheses marks on the keyboard. So I made all of my statements direct—just as if I were talking to you."

That same directness has characterized Helen's life throughout her sixty years, with a great deal of variety of living included. She was graduated from high school in 1914, then took voice lessons for two years while she taught school in Nebraska. Not satisfied with her singing, she entered a new field. She became a bank teller during World War I, after which she moved to a ranch in Idaho, and finally settled in California. Today she operates a bar, does all the work herself, and every week visits her aged mother, whom she helps support.

"I've had more ups and downs than I care to tell about," she says. "But all my life I have had an interest in the occult and the unseen, the hard to explain things about me," she says. "I was a student of astrology and became a palmist years ago. In fact I made my living entertaining in this field for several years."

Her study of astrology led to an interest in reincarnation, which she says she explored for her own satisfaction.

"All of this led me to a recognition of the biggest word in my vocabulary today," Helen says. "That word is WHY. Trying to find that answer is the main reason for my interest in people and what they do."

"My first intentional contact with homosexuals as a group was to determine if there was a pattern in their palms. My gradual integration with such groups has come through mutual affection and respect. I am at home with them."

Homosexual or not, everyone, it seems, has an immediate reaction to Helen. No in-between regard for this intensely active and perceptive woman is possible; it is a case of love her a lot or not at all. But readers of her book, "Gay Bar," will see at once what the reaction of the majority is.

"Everybody loves Helen," say those who know her. It's a safe prediction that sons and daughters, as well as mothers and fathers, will be infected with the same feeling for her after they read the book, too.

THE WOMAN WHO WROTE A LITTLE BOOK about her experiences running a Hollywood gay bar in the 1950s was born Helen Pyle in 1896. She graduated from high school in Hastings, Nebraska, where she played basketball and performed in choral and theatrical productions. Accompanying her photo in the senior yearbook: "She's all right but likes to chatter. If nothing worse, what does this matter?"

Helen Pyle, Hastings, Nebraska, 1915. Courtesy Caroline Branson Hammond and Russell Hammond.

While Helen was singing with a band several years after high school, she met Zebulon Branson, a World War army veteran, and they married in 1918. They soon left Nebraska to work on an Idaho ranch owned by Zeb's father. Their only child, Helen Caroline, was born there in 1920. Among other chores, Helen found herself cooking meals for the seasonal help.

Both ranch life and married life proved to be a trial for the couple, leading Helen to make a break for California, where her brother, Eddie, was working in Hollywood as a camera operator. One day in 1922 Helen set out from the ranch, pushing a milk-can cart loaded with luggage and child. A couple of miles down the road, she and Caroline reached the railroad line and headed for Los Angeles. Helen worked as a bank teller there, putting Caroline in a care home during the workweek and taking her out on weekends. Zeb joined them before long, employed as an engineer in the telephone industry. In the late 1920s Helen's widowed mother moved from Nebraska to Los Angeles to be near her daughter and son.

Helen Branson in winter hat on a Sunday stroll with her daughter, Caroline, at Westlake Park, Los Angeles, about 1925. Helen wrote on the back of the snapshot, "Best kodak I ever had of myself but that isn't saying much." Courtesy Caroline Branson Hammond and Russell Hammond.

Zeb Branson's income sustained the household comfortably until the early 1930s, when he got involved with another woman and told Helen that he wanted a divorce. "She was so upset about him going off and leaving her, she wouldn't take any money from him," Caroline recalled. "And thus we didn't have any money!" Uncle Eddie came through with gifts of cash and little luxuries that made a big difference for Helen and Caroline. Then a fashion-minded teenager at Hollywood High, Caroline remembers Eddie's gifts of five-dollar gold pieces and a good-looking sweater. "I'd never had any clothes," she said. "Times were tough; my mother couldn't earn a good living—she was always on the edge of something." In 1937 Caroline dropped out of high school to work as a stock girl in an upscale Hollywood dress shop, the start of her career in the fashion industry.

With her freethinking ways and longstanding interest in the occult, Helen was very much on the edge, even by Hollywood standards. By the late 1930s she found work as a palm-reading nightclub entertainer. In gypsy costume she drifted among tables at Lindy's on Wilshire Boulevard, taking the hands of late-night diners and explicating their features in the glow of her small flashlight. So began her gradual convergence with gay men. Eventually she was working as house mother and cook in a gay rooming house, then managing several gay bars owned by others. In 1952, a year after the California Supreme Court declared it legal for homosexuals to congregate in bars, Helen took over a small neighborhood tavern at 5124 Melrose Avenue and began operating her own gay bar in her own way.

Gay Bar

Introduction

Judge not that ye be not judged. For with what judgment ye judge, ye shall be judged: and with what measure ye mete, it shall be measured to you again. And why beholdest thou the mote in thy brother's eye, but considerest not the beam in thine own eye?

The Great Physician in Matthew 7: 1–3

In *Gay Bar* Helen Branson strikes a new note in homophile literature, for in it she accepts and appreciates homosexuals. When we discussed the book together, we were pleasantly surprised to find how thoroughly we agreed on so many points concerning this controversial subject. Therefore I am pleased and happy to set forth some of my views to accompany her book.

Homosexuals are human beings, too. They are interesting, real, unusual, creative, beauty-loving people, if one can get behind the mask of camping pretense and sham so many of them feel compelled to wear to protect their sensitive souls from the condemnation and hate leveled at them by a hostile, prejudiced, and uncomprehending society. It is my firm belief, based on years of experience working with many types and varieties of the clan in a psychiatric practice, that homosexuals have a definite place in society today as in the past, but they, themselves, must demonstrate their true worth by coming to know and accept themselves, thus releasing their potentials which are all too often blocked by their lack of self-confidence and reflected hostility. To my way of thinking, homophiles, both male and female, are really not so different from the rank and file of humanity except in their preference for a love object belonging to the same sex. It seems to me it is a matter of taste such as, "Do you prefer your coffee with cream and sugar or do you take it straight?"

Stereotyped thinking blocks progress in understanding these "different" people. Attempts to describe a "typical" homosexual become highly amusing because they appear in so many forms and, outside of the obviously exaggerated "swish" types, they are very difficult to detect, even among themselves. There are countless homophiles who are well-adjusted members of society, doing excellent work in many fields of art, business, industry, and the professions. They have skillfully masked their own "deviation" and pass undetected as accepted members of that very society which looks down the nose with scorn upon their more insecure and maladjusted brethren. Such shining examples of the brotherhood need never find their way to a psychiatrist's office but may be met socially and will reveal themselves only to someone they trust, someone who is wise. They often lead lonely lives and long for the good companionship of others who speak their own versatile language with so much quick repartee. Frequently they are as intolerant of their more maladjusted brothers as are heterosexuals. They shudder at the vulgar mannerisms of "gays" and "Nellies" as much as do "straight" people. The vast problem of alcoholism probably has its roots in homosexuality. There is a great need for homosexuals to understand themselves as well as to have heterosexuals understand them. Too many homosexuals court rejection.

I do not consider homosexuality to be a disease. Like Dr. Alfred Kinsey, I regard it as one of our mammalian heritages, of complex origins, so widespread in the animal kingdom that no serious student could consider it to be unnatural but merely a variation of commonly accepted sexual behavior. Any human being who suffers from pain, rejection by his fellows, overly strict authoritarian control, neglect, or over-indulgence, may develop neurotic or even psychotic conditions and need psychiatric help. Homosexuals are no exception. Even the best natured dog, if kicked around enough, may snarl and bite back. I regard objectionable mannerisms and social conduct of "queers" as neurotic expressions of their inward fears and hostilities and not due to their homosexuality *per se*. The rapidity with which such traits disappear in group therapy under the skilled guidance of trained non-critical leaders verifies this.

At this point I believe there should be a clarification of some of the terms in common use. Homosexuals—or perhaps the better term is "homophiles"—are people who prefer the love of members of their own sex. There are many other terms used such as sexual invert, pervert, deviate, the "third sex," "queer," or "gay." However, it should be understood that the terms "homosexual" and "gay" are not the same but overlap. Not all homosexuals are "gay." That term is applied especially to those who are just "coming out" or acknowledging their membership in a minority group. It seems that they wish to submerge themselves in a herd in which they adopt a common jargon like teenagers' "bop" and "jive" talk, thus allaying some of their fears. Since they have little awareness of their own individuality or originality and are lacking in self-confidence and self-acceptance, they gain a shallow identification with a group and find a welcome outlet for their resentments and hostilities toward a world which rejects them. Usually there is considerable hate released toward the parent or parents who failed to understand them. Thus "gays" may be considered homosexuals in adolescent rebellion. Much cruising is a search for the other self, a companion who can understand—not just sex—and much of their phrenetic love-making is a compulsive drive to find their elusive ego-ideal, which has generally been damaged by the same sex parent, while they have identified with the opposite sexed parent, but with resentment. In well organized and carefully moderated discussion groups there is the opportunity to understand themselves better, develop self-acceptance and the ability to stand alone, which helps them to become more integrated and more secure, thus daring to release more of their real selves. Such non-profit educational and research corporations as One, based on Carlyle's statement, ". . . a mystic bond of brotherhood makes all men one," the Mattachine Society and the Daughters of Bilitis are excellent examples of organized groups which are encouraging homosexuals to find themselves and their place in society. Their educational and research programs point the way for a new day for this outcast group of talented people. What opportunities for leadership there are here.

Of one thing we can be sure; like sex, homosexuality is here to stay. No amount of condemnation, criticism, entrapment or incarceration in penal and mental institutions can wipe out the fact of the existence of this tremendously large minority. There is so much secrecy connected with it that it is almost impossible to estimate the incidence of homosexuality. Since *Gay Bar* deals with male homosexuals it might be of interest to know how widespread the problem is. Dr. Kinsey (in *Sexual Behavior in the Human Male*, by Kinsey, Pomeroy & Martin; W. B. Saunders Co., 1948) found that at least 37% of the male population had had some homosexual experience between the beginning of adolescence and old age, which is more than one male in three that one passes on a city street. In the United States alone it has been estimated that there are between 12 million and 15 million homosexuals, based on the findings of Kinsey and other leading research experts. They are found among all races, all nationalities and all religious denominations—in every profession and every occupation. They are found in every city and town. It is reported that there are probably 200,000 in a city such as San Francisco. The social, economic, and venereal disease problems involved are staggering. Certainly such a widespread problem as this deserves much more careful study and evaluation than it has received heretofore. Ignoring the problem or condemning the homosexual does not solve the enigma and often makes it worse by bringing forth more overt hostility. It seems to me that the only way is to accept and appreciate the homosexual thus bringing forth his better side and encouraging him to accept a constructive place in society.

One of the major factors in understanding homosexuality is to clarify our knowledge of the nature of our own sexuality. It is regrettable that all too many people think of sex in terms of an absolute dichotomy: men are male and women are female. Yet it takes very little observation to perceive that every man is a mixture of maleness and femaleness. For an example in the physical realm: Even the toughest male has rudimentary breasts while even the most delicate female has a rudimentary penis. When we consider the more fluid emotional nature the mixtures become infinitely more complex; a male body may be inhabited by a very feminine psyche and vice versa. Nature does not deal strictly with blacks and whites for in between them spread all the colors of the rainbow. The same is true of sex. People simply cannot be divided into heterosexuals and homosexuals, either, for there are so many grades in between including bisexuals, attracted equally to either sex. Kinsey recognized this and proposed a 7-point linear rating scale for heterosexuality—homosexuality. However, the rigidity of this graph misses so much of the subtle blending of male and female traits as one observes them in individuals, either male or female, homosexual or heterosexual.

The continuum of nature is much better expressed in a clock-like diagram such as that devised by Gavin Arthur in his yet unpublished manuscript, "The Circle of Sex," in which one can easily find one's self some place on the circle. Such a *schema* clearly presents the blend of positive and negative or the *yang* and *yin* aspects which are used by the Chinese in the *tai-gitu* to symbolize the universal oneness of life. This symbol is pictured at the end of this introduction. It is well worth studying. Dr. Carl Jung (see *The Psychology of Jung* by Jacobi; Kegan Paul, Trench, Trubner & Co., 1942) makes a great deal of use of this symbol in his psychology. He also recognized the basic bisexuality of man in his use of the terms *anima*, the woman in man, and the *animus*, the man in woman. Studies such as these may help us gain a better appreciation of the gradient or dynamic blend we find throughout the world of nature. However, until we can release the repressed contents of our unconscious "minds" and give this hidden part of our natures the respect we grant our conscious minds, we have little chance of really understanding for we are held in the grip of our rigid thalamic thinking, the black and white thinking characteristic of the old animal-brain, also recognized as infantile thinking which is not true thinking at all but a primitive emotion-controlled reaction pattern observed in adult human beings who are dominated by the unconscious, or lower selves. It may be recognized by the repetitious, illogical statements which sound like a phonograph. When we are in the grip of such unreason we are incapable of using the fine discrimination of the higher brain centers and have no awareness of the compassionate intuitive understanding of the spiritual nature controlled by the higher Self, the inward authority, or God Self.

I doubt if the homosexual can be accepted in society until he learns to clear himself from the hate, prejudice and intolerance within himself. He must know himself and balance his own unruly nature before he can expect many others to understand him.

I am often asked why "straights" hate "gays" so much. This question brings right out into the open the primitive emotions aroused in so many people by the very mention of the subject of homosexuality. Most of us are so blind to our repressed animalistic urges that we may deny that we hate anyone yet we may be showing intolerance, persecution and overt acts of hostility toward members of our own family or toward minority groups. It comes as a shock to most of us when we finally realize that we are actually harboring such crude feelings which are subtly controlling our thoughts and actions. Despite our pride in the advancement of modern civilization, especially in the realm of science, we are still loath to explore that last dark continent, our own unconscious, loaded with so many undigested experiences and other unlovely things which keep us from realizing our rich potentials held prisoner in that underground world, as it were. Since we strongly resist facing that which is painful or unpleasant, could it be that all too many of us fear to face the homosexuality hidden within ourselves so we have to find a whipping boy or a scapegoat on which to vent our feelings of hostility?

Perhaps we simply are not brave enough to admit that *we* may have been harboring what we consider a loathsome thing (thanks to our Puritan ancestors) so we attack the "dirty" homosexual to cover up our own guilt and shame. Even leading psychiatrists do not seem to be free from this taint. Just read the titles of books dealing with the problems of the homosexual and ask yourself how these men must feel about it: titles such as *Homosexuality: Disease or Way of Life* by Dr. Edmund Bergler and *Is Homosexuality a Menace?* by Dr. Arthur Guy Matthews. Furthermore, when one reads these books one is tempted to ask, "Why does homosexuality threaten these men so much?" Yet they say they are not prejudiced! "Physician, heal thyself!"

There are many theories extant regarding the causative factors in homosexuality. Among them are the genetic, the endocrine, the sexual arrest, various psychological theories, and that of original sin. For those who are interested it would be well to read Donald Webster Cory's *The Homosexual in America* (Greenberg, 1951). At this time, however, it might be well to at least suggest the consideration of a new theory set forth very ably by Gina

Cerminara (*The World Within*, Wm. Sloane Associates, 1957), the reincarnation theory. She suggests that if man is a soul which lives many, many times in both male and female bodies, then this theory may shed considerably more light on the problem of homosexuality. If such sexual alternations do occur, it would certainly wipe out the absoluteness of cleavage between men and women. She cites case histories from the records of the famous clairvoyant Edgar Cayce.

My own research in deep psychotherapy with many homosexuals—using a type of meditation, *not* hypnosis—verifies this. Helen Branson concurs in this theory and believes that many of the behavior patterns of her own clients may be explained by their having been women in former lives.

Homosexuality is not a new problem but seems to have existed throughout the ages. But it has not always been considered a problem. Brief mention should be made here of the outstanding roles played by homosexuals in the past, notably in the Greek civilization and in medieval times when troubadours and court jesters played prominent parts in court life. These "fools," or *mattachines*, were clever men who were deeply involved in political intrigues. They were men of wisdom who dared to speak the truth in the face of stern authority, regardless of the consequences. Their significance is perpetuated today in such androgynous figures as Parsifal and the fool, Aleph, in the Tarot cards. Societies in which the homosexual's real ability was recognized and made use of are called the *Berdache*. It is heartwarming to hear that there are today anthropologists such as the Drs. Benedict, Beach, and Ford who are interested in such societies and it is discernible between the lines that some eminent archeologists such as Prof. Childe are interested in the re-exhumations of the *Berdache* cultural contributions.

Books such as G. Rattray Taylor's *Sex in History* (Vanguard Press, 1954) show quite clearly that there have been cycles of acceptance and rejection of the homosexual depending upon the dominance of a father- or mother-controlled religion. We seem to be coming into a mother-controlled cycle in which the attitude toward the homosexual is generally more permissive. Perhaps Helen Branson is a forerunner of the New Age. She impresses one with her wholesome, practical, forthright motherly ways. She is well portrayed by the hovering mother hen caricature in this book. She protects her "chicks" with wisdom and love. She is no "mom" who gives "smother love." Helen is a wise mother who exemplifies the rare combination of tender, sustaining, nourishing feminine type of love symbolized by the Oriental goddess of mercy, *Kwan-Yin*, combined with the firm, stern, disciplinary male type of love symbolized by the Japanese god *Fudo*. By this healthy combination Helen guides her boys and has such a harmonious atmosphere at her Gay Bar that she doesn't even have to ask Mr. John Law to help her keep order. She draws to her a high class clientele yet an excellent cross-section of gay fellows. And where else can they go? Bars are well known as gathering places for the lonely and maladjusted of all kinds. I am no admirer of bars as such, but I am practical and I recognize that they have their place in our society. There are so few private homes or social clubs available to homophiles that they are forced to go to bars for fun and companionship. Naturally they cluster in gay bars — and there are gay bars and Gay Bars and GAY BARS. Helen's is a very exceptional gay bar, for it is almost like a private club, thanks to her astuteness and keen understanding. Her unique supervision creates a wholesome atmosphere in which the creative potentials of her boys can be released in fun, good conversation, artistry and parties. She really listens to the problems of her boys. Aren't bartenders well known as the precursors of psychiatrists?

Helen Branson is a wise mother. May there be more like her!

Blanche M. Baker, M.D., Ph.D.

San Francisco, California

August 31, 1957

HELEN READ BLANCHE'S DRAFT INTRODUCTION for *Gay Bar* and had two of her boys at the bar read it as well. They raised their eyebrows at seeing Blanche liken Helen's love for her boys not only to that of two Oriental deities but also to that of "the Blessed Mother of the Catholics." Helen mailed off a quick note to publisher Hal Call that "perhaps the Catholics might resent the reference to the 'Blessed Mother' and maybe we better knock it out. Can't have the church on our necks." Never mind that Helen could not have been flattered by the comparison, given her disdain for organized religion. "Jehovah's Witnesses would ring the doorbell and she'd run them off by saying she was a witch," said Helen's grandson, Russ Hammond. "She would extol the virtues of Wiccanism to them and blow their minds."

San Francisco psychiatrist Blanche Montgomery Baker had been in private practice for about fifteen years when Hal Call invited her to read Helen's manuscript and write an introduction. Blanche was not Hal's first choice in his pursuit of a doctor's name to give the book an authoritative, scientific aura: At the top of his wish list was psychotherapist Albert Ellis, who viewed homosexuals as neurotic and favored helping them to become heterosexuals. Next on the list was Paul Gebhard, a successor of recently deceased sexologist Alfred Kinsey. Both had national name recognition. But Blanche Baker ended up getting the job, and it's hard to imagine a doctor's voice that would have better complemented Helen's.

"My stress is on self-acceptance," Blanche said, "—to learn to appreciate who and what you are and how to release your very own unique creativity in a discriminating and wholesome fashion. There are thousands of well-adjusted homosexuals leading busy useful lives. With a little encouragement there can be many more doing the same. I firmly believe that homosexuals have a very definite place in society today."

How startling these statements must have been to homosexuals in a time when it was bold simply to state that "homosexuals are people, too." Views like Blanche's were rarely encountered in print in the 1950s. Most prominent were male psychiatrists who, after psychoanalyzing a procession of distressed, cure-seeking homosexuals, published articles and books that described homosexuality as a neurotic disease. Publication of such books surged in the late 1940s and the 1950s, with titles like *Their Mothers' Sons*, *The Neurotic*, and *The Problem of Homosexuality*.

Viennese psychiatrist Wilhelm Stekel, a close associate of Freud, was a key figure in setting the tone through the first half of the twentieth century. "The homosexual neurosis is a flight back to one's own sex induced by a sadistic predisposition towards the opposite sex," he stated. Stekel was convinced that some homosexuals could be cured through psychoanalysis, but the patient had to "actively desire a change in his leaning" and persist willingly in treatment for a long time, often years, in order to achieve "adequate self-knowledge." Stekel disapproved of physicians and psychoanalysts who deemed a patient cured "when he is able to have normal coitus a few times." He insisted that a cure could be claimed only after the patient "falls in love with a suitable person of the other sex . . . in other words, when he learns to love in an adult manner."

Physicians throughout America built and fortified the case for psychopathology. "For nearly thirty years now I have been treating homosexuals, spending many hours with them in the course of their analyses," Edmund Bergler said in his book *Homosexuality: Disease or Way of Life?* "I can say with some justification that I have no bias against homosexuals; for me they are sick people requiring medical help." He stated, "*There are no healthy homosexuals.* The entire personality structure of the homosexual is pervaded by the *unconscious* wish to suffer; this wish is gratified by self-created *trouble-making*."

Blanche understood gay men's mental health problems to be more a result of their oppressed status than of their sexual orientation per se. "While I do not belong to the school of thought . . . which holds that homosexuality is some sort of disease," she wrote, "I do realize that homophiles are subject to neuroses and other forms of mental illness if they do not learn to clean out conflicts in their unconscious, accept themselves and make use of whatever individual abilities they may have."

The dominant view of "the homosexual problem"—a view that focused almost exclusively on male homosexuality—was that because of some conjunction of causes not yet fully understood, an individual had become established in a deviant, unhealthy sexual pattern. A determined effort should be made to effect a cure: help the individual adjust to a new sexual pattern that conformed to straight norms, at least on the surface if not more deeply. Common treatments included psychotherapy, drugs, electroshock, brain surgery, hormones, and hypnosis. Most psychotherapists realized that the "cured" person would be unlikely to ever escape all traces of the deviant pattern, but by making a convincing show of normalcy—getting married and having children, in particular—he would join the ranks of "apparent cures."

Many psychotherapists enjoyed very good incomes from helping homosexuals work toward "heterosexual adjustments." One man's psychoanalytic odyssey involved sessions with his doctor six days a week for two years, then five days a week for another three years. This enabled him to marry and father two children. Through the decades of his marriage he drank and smoked heavily and sought out-of-town sex with men. In his mid-70s, his wife dead, he began to identify publicly as gay.

Psychoanalysis led a 25-year-old naval officer, "a practicing homosexual with no heterosexual interests of any kind," and his doctor to conclude that his deviation was due to fear of his mother and women in general. They decided that this fear was the result of a traumatic incident in infancy: while nursing at his mother's breast, his sexual feelings were aroused and he choked as a result of gulping milk. Due to this greater self-understanding, "his fear of women was abolished. He married, had children and wrote to the psychiatrist that 'marriage is wonderful.'"

A psychotherapist described the apparent cure of "a particularly difficult case . . . a man aged thirty years . . . who complained that he had never had any attraction to women, but periodically he had a strong impulse to have anal intercourse with men. . . .When last heard of, a year after cessation of treatment, he was living happily with his wife and appeared to be completely normal."

To appear to be normal was key in 1950s America. Even scientific tests of mental health were likely to be little more than measures of conformity. And so it's no surprise that early allies of homosexuals came from the ranks of heterosexual nonconformists. Like Helen, Blanche Baker believed in reincarnation, telling a homophile audience that she had been a gay man in most of her previous lives. She endorsed a theory put forth by a popular re-incarnation proponent: After several lifetimes as one sex, it can be difficult for a person to function physically, psychologically, and socially as the other sex. "Homosexuality can be the result" of this "psychological hang-over." A lesbian endorsed this view in her letter to *ONE* magazine, insisting that reincarnation was the most plausible explanation for homosexuality — "the transition period of leaving a male body in one life and coming into a female body in the next life, and vice-versa."

Blanche's husband, William Baker, was a social worker and grapholo-gist whose handwriting analysis and counseling work dovetailed with his wife's psychotherapy practice: "A figure-eight lower loop is the sign of the Lesbian. . . . A circle dot over an I is the sign of the seeker for beauty. . . . A tee crossed low shows a person interested in physical satisfaction." Together they specialized in group therapy and psychodrama. The Bakers had no children, and, like Helen, their social circle included many homosexuals.

"Dr. B. is guilty of identifying with her patients," Blanche replied to a chastising letter from another San Francisco psychiatrist. "She believes that democratic procedures are desirable in human relations. Thus she dares to violate the code of the Mystery-Man Cult of Medicine and to practice the art of healing by being a kindly, friendly, motherly sort of doctor (or teacher) who practices brotherhood, preaches self-acceptance and even en-joys the companionship of 'dirty' homosexuals. . . . Since most people who seek my help, including homophiles, are basically hurt children who are still controlled by their emotional natures, . . . I have developed the art of communicating with each individual at the various levels at which he func-tions. . . . I find that much non-verbal communication is required, includ-ing the warmth and affection a wise mother will give her hurt babe. A good sense of humor is valuable in bringing the shattered personality together to produce a more integrated, happy, creative and efficient human being."

The shock of having a female schoolmate fall in love with her at a young age opened Blanche's eyes to homosexuality. Having a father who helped her find books on the subject enabled Blanche to be supportive of her schoolmate. The books she read in the 1920s presented homosexual-ity as mental illness, but Blanche's years of psychiatric work with both

Dr. Blanche M. Baker (1906–60) with William F. Baker, 1957. Courtesy ONE National Gay and Lesbian Archives.

homosexuals and heterosexuals led her to discard the idea that homosexuals were necessarily mentally ill. Her conclusions were in accord with those of psychologist Evelyn Hooker, whose groundbreaking research in the 1950s found no difference in psychological adjustment between homosexual and heterosexual men.

The hodgepodge of theories on the cause of homosexuality was an astonishing litany: "a biological anomaly; hereditary defect; an immature form of skeletal development; endocrine imbalance; a child from degenerate stock; pre-Oedipal aggression and the oral trauma of weaning; the castration complex; mother fixation; identification or rivalry with the parent of the opposite sex; faulty training during elimination learning; emotional excesses from a maladjusted upbringing; early dominance by one parent; absence of male influences in the home; regression to or fixation at an earlier libidinal level; ignorance in matters connected with sex; seduction during childhood or adolescence; early onset of adolescence; painful sex experiences at puberty; segregation of the sexes during adolescence; fear of the opposite sex caused by feelings of inferiority; restraints on pre-marital heterosexual intercourse; lack of sexual success with women."

Doc Baker was impatient with the fixation on causes and cures. Stop being afraid and hiding behind a mask, she urged homosexuals. Stop taking out your resentments on yourself instead of those responsible for them. Discover your unique potential, combining as you do both male and female attributes, and step forth to fill your special places in society. "Many creative fields lie ahead of you *if* you will but stop despising yourselves, stop being ashamed and start creating a place for yourselves on this earth," she stated. "It is not inconceivable. There were societies in the past which allowed homosexuals their place."

But Blanche saw no special place in society for "gays," "queers," "Nellies"—terms that represented for her "the obviously exaggerated 'swish' types" who wore a "mask of camping pretense and sham." She contrasted them with their homosexual brethren who, having "skillfully masked their own 'deviation,'" were able to go about their lives largely undetected by straights. Blanche noted that many homosexuals shared her scorn for the "vulgar mannerisms" of affected "swish." She maintained that if these flamboyant ones could be helped toward emotional maturity, their objectionable mannerisms and conduct would fade away. In disapproving of homosexual men wearing masks to accentuate their feminine characteristics while approving of masks that helped them to butch it up, Blanche was entirely in line with prevailing attitudes among homophiles.

To Blanche, homosexuality originated in a complex mix of environmental and hereditary factors. Like many of her colleagues, she viewed the mother influence as a key element: "Since the mother is the first female every child encounters, and since this mother has most to do with the shaping and training . . . of the child's body and behavior patterns, all children, homo or not, tend to resent the mother and to carry hidden hostility for her, while she in turn may secretly feel that the child has thwarted her personal ambitions."

In Blanche's view, the flamboyantly effeminate behavior of some homosexual men resulted from their accumulated hostilities finding campy expression "in a bewildering pattern of speech, mannerisms, actions and interests." She believed that "when hostile attitudes toward mother-figures can be freely released there is a marked reduction in the behavior patterns mentioned above and the homophile becomes more accepting of his own feminine nature. He tends to find more agreeable work and companionship, and as he accepts himself he gets along better with mother-figures."

Blanche went along with some of the prevailing mainstream ideas about how men and women ought to present and conduct themselves socially, but she was much too familiar with the realities of the human psyche to put people into boxes. To Blanche, even Kinsey's seven-point hetero-to-homo spectrum was of limited value because it pertained to sexual activity, not sexual orientation per se, and it did not consider the distinctive blend of feminine and masculine traits "as one observes them in individuals, either male or female, homosexual or heterosexual."

Understanding human types in the context of continuums rather than categories, Blanche was a fan of Gavin Arthur's intriguing "circle of sex" model, explained in his 1962 book *The Circle of Sex*, published by Pan-Graphic, with an introduction by Blanche. Gavin Arthur stated that sex could not be understood in terms of "a straight line ranging from pure male on the one end . . . to pure female on the other end." In his clock-like diagram he attempted to present in twelve types "the infinitely varied sexual makeup of human beings, seen in all its shades and gradations."

Gavin Arthur, a San Francisco astrologer and occultist, provided astrological counseling in close association with Blanche, just as Blanche's husband provided graphological counseling. Replying to a man in his late twenties who sent a lengthy letter detailing his uncertainty about whether he was gay or straight, Blanche noted that his handwriting "shows many of the characteristics of an overt homosexual. Using Gavin Arthur's 'Circle of Sex,' I would classify you as a quasi-homosexual—in other words, one who is bi-sexual, but more homosexual than bi-sexual."

Blanche's connection with Gavin Arthur suggests an explanation for her assertion that "the vast problem of alcoholism probably has its roots in homosexuality." Discussing Gavin Arthur's acquaintance with Alfred Kinsey, Blanche stated that the two men agreed "that much of the alcoholism for which Americans are famous is largely due to sex repressions, the result of Puritanism." In this light, Blanche was apparently suggesting a link between alcoholism and internal conflict about one's sexual disposition, the homosexual component in particular.

Surveying American culture in the 1950s, Gavin Arthur decried "the almost feverish demand that all men dress alike in one way, all women dress alike in another—all men think like 'men,' all women think, act, talk in a stereotyped 'feminine' way." Speaking on a 1958 radio broadcast, "The Homosexual in Our Society," Blanche foresaw changes: "We are coming into a period where there seems to be more enlightenment, more awareness of the individual's needs to express himself as long as he doesn't bring sorrow or harm to other people."

In 1959 and 1960 Blanche wrote "Toward Understanding," a monthly column for *ONE*, in which she responded to letters from readers. The magazine received far more letters than its small staff had ever been able to handle. America's first advice columnist for homosexuals quickly developed a devoted following. "Within the topmost glitter of the diamond is Dr. Baker and her superhuman effort to impart help for the troubled in warmth and kindness and understanding," Mr. L. wrote from New Orleans. "'Toward Understanding' could not have been better named, unless you retitled it 'The Glow from Dr. Baker's Heart.'"

Readers were hungry not only for Blanche's thoughtful replies but also for the letter-writers' candid self-disclosures, offering windows into the struggles, successes, and self-understandings of others like themselves. In one letter, a 23-year-old described his childhood difficulties due to being effeminate, his frustrated loves as an adolescent and young man, and his persistent feelings of inferiority, guilt, and loneliness. "Please tell me," he wrote, "does a homosexual have the right to love and be loved as any other human? Is it a crime to love a man with all my heart? Is it wrong to have relations with a man? . . . Will I have to live my life crying and suffering forever?"

Putting a colorful twist on the idea of homosexuality as part of "our mammalian heritage," another reader broke his long silence to describe childhood sex-play with other boys: "With the coming of spring, we took to the deep woods and the pure unaltered animal in us came out. We began to experiment with our sex organs and came up with such games as 'cow,' with three different versions. First we played it with some of us being the cows and some the farmers who milked the 'cows.' Then came cow and calf, and therein we found the physical pleasure of oral sex. Then came the third natural form, cow and bull. All these forms were mutual. No one ever objected, unless he thought he wasn't getting in on the games as much as the next boy."

Blanche thanked the writer for his "wholesomely humorous" letter: "I wish that everyone would realize that there is no need to feel ashamed or disgusted with activities that are so natural and so universal. The fact that you kept silence so many years demonstrates that there are deep-seated fear reactions and feelings of guilt springing from deep-rooted puritanical teachings: tendencies to repress or hide certain activities that are quite normal." In her view, those who saw homosexuality as a crime against nature did not know nature.

"I am convinced," a young man wrote, "that being a homosexual is not a handicap, sickness or anything else, but is instead a very definite blessing. Let me explain.

"Up until January of this year I was completely normal, as it were, or so I thought. I was the leader of a rough and tumble group of young men, participating in sports, hot rod races, and general corner drug store antics.

"Yet all this time I seemed incomplete, unfinished—something from my life was missing. I began losing interest in the corner gang, and instead began searching, searching for something. I would get up each day with the prayer that I might find my missing part.

"On January 18th it happened. It was Sunday and late at night. A friend of mine had invited me to go for a ride with him in his car. We drove to a desolate, sandy beach; there was a bright moon. He slid over next to me and put his arms around me. Then we began talking about sex and he began asking me about my sexlife. There was little to tell. I felt I knew him a hundred years. I admit I was shocked when I felt him fondle me; but I loved it and asked him to go farther. The next half hour opened my eyes to a new world. At long last I had found what I was looking for.

"Now I walk with a smile on my face, a gleam in my eye, and a song in my heart. I've found my place in the world and I love it. I have been blessed. So tell your readers not to be afraid; never a more wholesome group of wonderful people ever lived."

Blanche's reply was affirming but cautionary: "I am sure you will find a happier adjustment in life by accepting your true nature. Thus, instead of putting so much of your vital energy into building smoke screens to hide behind, you can apply this same creative energy into working out a truly artistic sexual routine based on mutual interests and understanding friendships. Thus you could build a truly happy, creative life with someone whom you can respect and cherish. I'd love to hear what you have to say about it all a year from now. Remember that you have had a fortunate experience but not all homos are angels any more than all heteros are devils. Discrimination is important in all aspects of life. Just now you are wearing rose-colored glasses!"

Foreword

This is how it happened. Over a year ago I had dinner with my friends Faye and Barro. After an imaginative feast we sat in the den talking ceramics, listening to records and discussing events in my bar.

Faye said, 'You should write a book.'

I grinned at her. 'Me? Write a book?'

The suggestion stayed with me. After much thought I mapped a course. I bought a tape recorder and talked my ideas into it. I engaged a ghost writer and we were in BIG production! When I received the manuscript I was very unhappy. The writer had not shown my attitude, which is the most important part. So I scrapped the whole book as she had written it, and started from scratch.

I am the first to say that this is not a smoothly constructed volume, but what I tell is true. For obvious reasons, I have substituted names in every case.

If this book helps any parent to understand his boy and if any gay boy sees himself more clearly because of what I have written, then this book has a reason for existing.

Helen P. Branson

Hollywood, California

June 1957

Gay Bar

1

'well, get you, girl . . .'

I own a homosexual bar. In the nomenclature of the homosexual, it is called a Gay Bar.

My appearance does not make you think of me as a bar owner. My demeanor could remind you of your sixth grade teacher or the librarian in the Maple Street branch library. I am what is called heavy set, have silver hair, blue eyes, and walk in a positive manner. If you met me away from my business, my conversation would be about herbs or my grandson or nutrition or ESP but not about the price of beer wholesale nor the recent burglary at the bar.

The average heterosexual or straight person is not aware that bars catering to this group are in existence. Any large city has many of them. Some cater to both male and female deviates and if a stranger wanders into one of these, he does not realize that there is anything strange. Other bars, such as mine, welcome the gay men only. The newcomer's first reaction is to wonder where the women are, but he is not conscious of any difference other than that.

There are caste levels in this group and there are contrasts in the bars also. The popular conception of a homosexual is that he is a male who is limp-wristed, who arches his eyebrows if you look closely, wears makeup. This is true of a minority group and there are bars where these congregate.

These fellows are often shunned by the others because they are exhibition-ists. The majority of this larger group look and act like any heterosexual. They walk in fear of exposure and loss of job. They are fond of female company, have charming manners, date girls, and on the surface lead so-called normal lives. Many of this larger group never go near a gay bar. They have home parties or go to popular night clubs. My bar is unique in having patrons from this latter group only. This is intentional.

When I started the bar over four years ago, I maintained that there were enough gay fellows who wanted a quiet place to meet other gay fellows for an evening of social drinking and conversation to make a fair living and this has been true. My group is composed of professional men, business executives, owners of businesses, both large and small, and many from the motion picture industry. I have many designers, decorators, and artists. Television is represented here, and the stage. There is a sprinkling of com-posers and writers.

Others with less spectacular occupations are here too. Joe, one of my patrons, drives a bus. Hal is a die cutter in a large concern. Lee is the head of the service department of an automobile agency and is really 'butch.' Curt owns a dump truck and gets contracts for carrying dirt from new building sites. Bank clerks and stenographers are part of the group. Every one is clean, polite, and thoughtful.

As I work behind the bar I hear bits of conversation that range from telling a cute story to the description of a new movie set. Two fellows are deep in a discussion over costs of starting a new gift shop. Someone else tells me he has expanded his drapery business from one shop in a rented building to his own building and two branch shops. A boy who recently took on the job of running a new ice skating show spent many hours sitting at a back table working out acts for the show. He almost fell asleep one night from exhaustion. Costume check-ups, rehearsals, scenery, and interviews with skaters were almost too much. His mother knows he is gay and when she visits him she always makes a trip to the bar.

If someone says, 'Have you been to Helen's,' the answer can often be, 'No, where's that?' The querist has to give detailed directions for finding it, since the outside is very, very inconspicuous. The building is one story. It has been divided in two parts, the other side housing a small café. The large windows on my side have been painted a solid color and the only clue that the place is in operation is the neon sign over the door. When I go in at night I turn that on and I am open for business. The front door is paneled glass but from the outside one sees only a brown shade. The inside of the windows and door are covered by matchstick bamboo curtains.

My side of the building is adjacent to a service station which closes at seven o'clock, my opening time. We use the large lot for parking. Most of the customers drive in there and come in the side door. Since the neighborhood is not of the best, we are glad to avoid foot traffic. On a busy night the parking lot is full and I go to the door occasionally to make sure the driveways are not blocked.

If you came in the front door, you would first face a louvered screen of varnished redwood, and looking around that, you would see a long bar which seats seventeen persons. The back bar is old fashioned dark wood. I have resisted three years' persistent effort on the part of the boys for a change to a more modern one. I like it old fashioned, and anyway I tell them, 'It's my money you are trying to spend.'

I take lots of kidding about my demand for bargains.

A couple of years ago we needed a new decor. I spotted a bargain in Philippine mahogany panels, bought them, and put them on the walls myself. I had a badly pounded thumb to prove it. These panels are six feet high. I finished the top with strips of molding and waxed them. From the top of the paneling to the drop ceiling is a painted surface of rose beige. Several customers pitched in on the night we are closed and painted it for me.

Between the bar counter and the front windows, in rather close quarters, is a small pool table which at present is very popular. The two players usually have a large audience and the free advice and cheers make this a hilarious part of the bar. Opposite the counter is a group of booths with small round tables and over them is a long and narrow horizontal window. It is frosted and has a row of small pottery containers for plants. These do not get much sun through the frosted glass and the plants have to be replaced often.

As I face this window I can see light reflections as cars turn into the parking lot. This means more customers. The back bar has a mirror in the center with a shelf on each side. Two chrome cocktail shakers have been made into lamps with cone-shaped shades. At each end on the back bar are snacks. Pretzels, potato chips, nuts, and hot sticks, the customers' name for pepperoni.

About half the back wall has been cut out, making a former kitchen into a part of the main room. A bowling machine occupies half of this ell and a screen made of Venetian blinds hides stacks of beer cases. In a corner of the main room next to the ell are a curved bench and a large table. Behind this seat in the corner is a long narrow lighting fixture in front of which stands an attractive branch of manzanita. We have a planter at the base of it and philodendron growing over it. Add a jukebox by the front door, a cigarette machine toward the back, and you have a picture of the bar.

The bar, I think, can be compared to a club. When one of my boys brings in a new customer he introduces him to me immediately and I in turn introduce the new member to others in the bar. This puts everyone at ease. The hum of conversation beneath the juke box music is very gratifying to me. I'll confess that part of the hum is my voice. Everyone knows that the only way to get another bottle of beer is to interrupt my talk by dropping a coin on the bar. A newcomer who does not know of this system may sit with an empty bottle and an empty glass until his neighbor tells him what to do.

Some customers wander around talking to everyone. Others stay in one spot quietly watching what goes on. At one corner of the bar a huddle and occasional bursts of laughter tell me that some new stories are in circulation. If I am not too busy, I listen and try to come back with one, just to keep my hand in.

One evening two serious-faced ones were sitting in a booth. They were in deep conversation. One motioned to me to come over. When I got a minute I went around the end of the bar and sat with them.

Neal had a problem.

'Do you know anyone who comes in here who knows my type of business?'

'You have a printing concern, don't you, Neal?'

He nodded.

'What do you want him to do?'

He thought for a minute.

'I'll start him at $1.75 an hour, Helen. That is more than a shipping clerk usually gets, but I want him to know something about the business, so that I can push him into a job that is coming up soon. I want someone from here, and if you recommend him I feel he will be stable.'

I took Neal's phone number and promised to keep on the lookout.

Many times positions have been filled that way.

The other side of the story is when someone has been fired, or has quit, or the firm he has worked for has folded and he is looking for a job. I may send him to one of my customers who has an employment agency or I may know of a job that is open. Soon he will be busy again. I know this does not sound very much like a bar, but it's fun that way.

I do all the work myself. The bar is open six days a week and seven hours a day. I am in the bar one day a week, in the day time, to receive merchandise and at that time I give it a good scrubbing and polishing. Sometimes I hire someone to help me and we really take it apart. We use the vacuum cleaner on the bamboo curtains, we pull all the benches away from the wall, we wax the mahogany paneling and wax the back bar and counter. Once in a while I replant the vines that are under the window.

I make a satisfactory living and since I am sixty years old, I am happy not to have long hours. I'm also happy to be my own boss, even if I do drive myself more than anyone ever drove me.

As I've said more than once, 'I've never had it so good.' I bask in the warmth of the genuine affection I receive. Every holiday is an excuse for someone to bring me a gift and many gifts appear without a holiday to justify them. At the last anniversary party for the bar the 'loot' was so great that I said I felt that I had been passing up a good racket and that I thought I would have to celebrate Bastille Day. This was good for a laugh. Almost the only item I buy retail is food. And magazines.

All this cheerful talk about the bar is only one side of the homosexual life. These people have problems, many of them, and they cannot talk of them to anyone except someone in the group.

I have problems because of the type of bar I own. But anyone who owns a business has problems and I will take mine and be happy.

HELEN'S REMARK THAT "these people have problems" is great understatement. Most straights and even many gays viewed "the homosexual problem" as a predicament of a modern untouchable caste: millions of men and women whose lives were irredeemably at odds with, and a threat to, authentic manhood and womanhood. And this in an era when, as one psychiatrist put it, "non-conformism is the major, perhaps the only, sin of our time."

After the upheavals of the Depression and World War II, the collective mentality was intent on returning to an idealized normalcy, getting women out of the workplace and back into the home, reasserting men's authority. Fitting in meant getting married, producing children, behaving like a man or woman ought to. As Donald Webster Cory noted, "upholders of the official morality are always casting suspicion on anyone who is not happily married or is not an ardent woman-chaser."

Alfred Kinsey's revelations intensified and complicated this culture of conformism. His books on the sexual behavior of American men and women were published in 1948 and 1953, respectively. Widely read and reported on, they revealed many startling things, one of which was that homosexuality was much more common than many wished to imagine. Along with the looming threat of Communism and the nuclear arms race, and the intensification of "the Negro problem" as blacks organized against segregation, the unveiling of an extensive homosexual problem was hugely unsettling to the American psyche.

A result was the demonization of homosexuals. For several decades they had been simply sick and sinful curiosities. Now, since the public understood that homosexuals were numerous, without knowing for sure who was and who wasn't, they were lumped in with Communists as an insidious threat to American society. In 1950 President Eisenhower issued an executive order barring sexual perverts from federal government jobs. Psychiatrist Edmund Bergler warned that Kinsey's findings would be "politically and propagandistically used against the United States abroad, stigmatizing the nation as a whole in a whisper campaign."

American magazines and newspapers of the 1950s were often sensationalistic in handling the topic of homosexuality. A twenty-year-old college student's letter to a newspaper advice columnist conveyed his "desperate need" of her counsel concerning his college friend: "Bob is several years older than I, and is very mature for one so young. I admire him greatly and respect him—that is, until this past week, when I learned that he is homosexual. He even seems a bit proud that he is this way. . . . I realize that a person must be broadminded in this day and age; and that this is some sort of psychological sickness in Bob, and that I should look upon it as such. But right now I am terribly confused."

The columnist's reply: "Let's not get so broadminded that we can't make a cleancut saving distinction between psychological sickness, on the one hand, and downright addiction to vice on the other hand. If your friend Bob were only and simply psychologically sick, he would be shamed and anguished by his deviate tendencies; and desperately hopeful that a cure might be found, to restore him to self-respecting normalcy. As it happens, Bob's boastful manner, and your panic, indicate that he is trying to win you as a victim, or a convert to his brand of misconduct. So I think it more accurate to call him vicious, rather than merely sick." The columnist advised the fellow to "give Bob's 'friendship' the axe" before he found himself "isolated from the healthy herd, and kidnapped, as it were, into [a] halfworld of furtive abnormality."

In 1955 a Minneapolis newspaper columnist published a letter from a local father whose twenty-year-old son had dropped his girlfriend and "began an association with a strange group of fellows." A private detective hired by the father discovered that it was "a large group of active homosexuals." The wayward son was sent to a psychiatrist, who assured the parents that their son was normal and had just fallen in with the wrong group. The son soon resumed his previous life, "completely ashamed" of his wayward venture. "I don't have the answer," the columnist said, "but I do have the initial warning that should alert every last one of us to a social danger in our midst. It happened to a father right here in Minneapolis. He was courageous enough to act. He was also astute enough to sense the evil."

It would prove to be a big year for sensing homosexual evil. In September 1955 twenty men were arrested in Sioux City, Iowa, and incarcerated in a special "sexual psychopath" ward at a mental hospital until they were deemed cured after about six months. November 1955 brought the beginnings of the infamous homosexual panic in Boise, Idaho, with the *Idaho Daily Statesman* stoking the hysteria. "In the early 1950s," said journalist John Gerassi, "thousands of people were calling the *Statesman* or the police or the local FBI office to denounce an acquaintance, a neighbor, an enemy, even a friend, as a Communist. In 1955, they were denouncing homosexuals." Dozens of men were arrested in Boise, with sentences ranging from probation to life imprisonment.

Antihomosexual initiatives throughout the country prompted many gay men to move to Los Angeles and other major cities. Although these locales offered greater anonymity and more opportunities to connect with other gays, they were hardly safe havens. The Los Angeles Police Department was virulently antihomosexual. One lesbian likened being gay in Los Angeles to "being on the outskirts of civilization. It wasn't any easier to be gay in L.A. in those days than it would have been in Amarillo, Texas, or South Bend, Indiana."

If only this woman could have been a regular at Helen Branson's bar on Melrose Avenue, a few blocks east of RKO and Paramount Studios. It's hard to imagine a gay man moving to Hollywood, connecting with Helen, and not finding it at least a little easier to be gay, if only because of Helen's community-fostering social club. Open six days a week from 7 p.m. to 2 a.m., the bar was a closely monitored and controlled space, Helen's savvy honed by years of managing gay establishments. She demanded that her boys introduce newcomers to her upon arrival. If the newcomer passed her scrutiny, Helen introduced him to the others, and everyone could relax and carry on. By maintaining close control over who could inhabit her space and become one of her boys, she provided a relatively safe, commodious living room. That her boys showered her with gifts at parties celebrating the anniversary of the bar's opening confirms that Helen's was a very unusual establishment.

"Especially in the larger cities, a good many homosexuals are habitual visitors at various certain bars and lounges," J. D. Mercer explained in *They Walk in Shadow*. "Many such places, serving as unofficial clubs, cater only to homosexual trade. . . . Male and female homosexuals seldom frequent the same places. The one group resents the intrusion of the other rather more than they dislike the advent of sight-seeing 'normal' visitors. It is in such resorts that these confirmed homosexuals meet friends, hear the gossip of their submerged gay world, and occasionally find new acquaintances who will invariably be regarded as possible lovers unless one or the other of them is 'engaged'—that is, in the argot, engaged in a strictly confined affair with another person."

Helen's remark on "the hum of conversation beneath the juke box music" is amplified by Cory's observations: "Gay bars! In a sense the description is fitting, for here is a gaiety, a vivacity, that is seldom seen in other comparable taverns, nightclubs, bars, and inns. There is no craning of necks as a bored audience watches a wrestling match on a television screen. Instead, music comes forth unceasing, usually from a nickelodeon. The audience talks to the rhythm, drinks to the rhythm, hums and breathes the air of the music, and looks around as the door opens to see who has just entered. . . .

"'Play that song over again!'

"'Who's got some nickels for the juke box?'

"The music starts and some songs seem to be extremely popular that evening. If one were able to obtain a report on the music at the other gay bars, the similarity of taste would be striking. Everywhere the same song seems to have taken hold. . . . Then the song disappears, not as quickly as from general popularity, and its place of preeminence in every gay bar is assumed by another."

"The atmosphere is generally more relaxed, carefree, and lighthearted than elsewhere," Donald Webster Cory and John LeRoy observed. "A party is in the air and a mood of merriment prevails. . . . The conversation is often in the gay vernacular and centers around the gossip and talk of romances made and broken; of previous encounters and adventures, real or fantasied; of theater, fashion, interior design, music, art, literature, and sports in which they participate."

A Hollywood newspaper columnist stated, "It should come as no surprise that the cinema hamlet is a traditional mecca for homosexuals. . . . They came here for a kind of social acceptance. And they found it." A sensationalistic little paperback, *The Third Sex,* observed: "In Hollywood you may find one a writer and the other a scenic artist or musician, or technician; but, whatever their profession or trade may be, you may rest assured they are tops. It has been said that pictures could not be made if it were not for the Hollywood Lavender boys and their colossal artistic minds. They are masters at decorating, stage settings, wardrobe designing, make-up, posture and rhythm; and all Hollywood knows this, too."

Helen's description of her patrons suggests that many Hollywood lavender boys passed her inspection, along with an array of fellows in "less spectacular" vocations. But Helen's boys were not of the pronouncedly limp-wristed, eyebrow-arching, makeup-wearing type. Helen's affection for gay men was reserved for those who could pass as straight, more or less, and for whom doing so mattered. A bar in which these more conformity-minded fellows would feel safe and comfortable could not also accommodate obvious queens carrying on shamelessly.

2

'. . . don't scream at your mother . . .'

Everyone has his problems. He may not like his job, or he is paying for a house or he is starting in business for himself or he has to get a new car. These problems are always with us. The homosexual has other problems that have started when he was young and that remain with him today. He cannot talk them over with those close at home, in fact he would not know how to begin.

The boy who is basically homosexual realizes at an early age that he is different from the other kids. He often enjoys doing the things that are called sissy. He may help his mother about the house, for he is often her favorite or her only child. He feels different inside. Sometimes in these early teens he is introduced to sexual experimentation by others his own age, but this experience does not necessarily make him into a homosexual. That exploration among boys is the rule rather than the exception. He may reach college days or later before he is really introduced to homosexual activities that impress him.

In the meantime he has been going around with girls. Because of his sensitive nature and because he is so neat and polite he may be very popular with them. He is critical of their appearance but he has ideas for them in color combinations and hairdos and they LOVE it. If the girl is interested in a few kisses he will accommodate her. He is not as aggressive as he is responsive. At this stage a wise adult might detect the tendency toward gay life and by adroit questions and sympathetic talk, help him to face this trait. More often his adoring mother is secretly delighted that he is not too interested in girls and that she is to have him with her that much longer.

I am reminded of Frances Ann Kay. She was left with Jan to care for from his babyhood. Times were tough. His earliest memories are of the struggle she made to keep them housed and fed. She did the gardening after coming home from work and in Jan's words, 'She was the man of the family.'

'She would be digging around the rose bushes,' he continued, 'and would tell me to go in and get dinner. She went to work to support us. I went to school and did the house work. It was the only way out.'

Eventually Jan told her he was gay. It was quite a shock. It took her weeks of thinking to accept this but after she did accept it she took a very amusing stand. If she could accept this side of her son, so should everyone else. She was quite candid about the whole thing. Finally Jan had a little talk with her.

'We don't tell *everyone* about this, Mother. This is something that most people don't understand and don't want to accept.'

She stopped volunteering this information about Jan but she does not back down when remarks are made. I think she's terrific.

Other boys do not have this problem solved so pleasantly.

Ken, who hails from Baltimore, is an example. He told his mother that he was going to move from home.

'Where are you going to move?' she asked.

'I am moving in with Jimmie,' he replied in his outspoken way.

'I am in love with him.'

This bombshell started a flood of angry words and tears. An hour later Ken had his possessions in bags and boxes and into the car.

Later they reached a friendly basis but she has never accepted him as he is. Her letters have small references to his way of living, showing a hope that he will get over this foolish idea and marry.

John Bailey's problem is one that many, many gay fellows have. He lives a lie. It keeps him constantly on guard. He owns his own home, he has a fine position as a technician, owns a nice car and his mother lives with him. She has a small independent income so she is not a burden that way. But she wants to live his life. His father is dead and all her interest is centered in John.

She thinks he should marry and he has to be alert to remember which girl he is supposed to be in love with at this time. He refers to me, Helen, often. I am said to be his girl friend's chum.

He has to do what so many of the boys have to do. That is, watch his speech and be ready with a quick explanation if he does let something slip. After many years, he has become accustomed to thinking and living in two different worlds. One world is his job and his home life with his mother and the other world is his association with other gay fellows and his love for Bob.

His mother thinks that when he sees Bob several evenings a week that they are double dating with girls.

She wonders why they don't ever bring the girls out to the house to meet her and she lives in hope that he will marry soon. Of course he has to change his girl friend's name often, so his mom will not think he is getting serious about one girl.

My sympathy goes to him, because Love, the greatest thing in any one's life has to be hidden. His problem is that he not only cannot want what is thought of as a normal home life, but that he has to hide what he does want from public knowledge or be a target of abuse.

Fred, who has the same setup, with the additional factor of a sharp sister who lives in the house with his mother and him, has become an alcoholic and is developing an intense persecution complex because of the strain. His sister's pointed questions and his straight-laced, puritanical boss have him in a crossfire that is proving too much for him.

The sad part is that he is excellent in his field, hard to replace, and his mother would never get over the shock of it all. If public opinion were not as it is, he would not have this constant fear of exposure. It is disheartening to know that he cannot help it. He is a basic homosexual. He cannot change his attitude any more than I can change the color of my eyes.

There is one group of people who accept gay people as they are. In fact they are not even curious. Any one's sex life is his own problem.

I am referring to the creative arts. You may say, 'They are all homosexuals anyway.' This is not true. Writers, actors, composers, painters are so interested in creative ideas, either their own or others', that they are not too concerned with private lives. Of course the playwright will write about you, but he has no personal curiosity about your life. The creative artist recognizes in gay folk their rebellion against set forms of thinking. He is drawn to them.

I see this exchange of ideas often. As I work along the bar I hear much conversation about color contrasts, or different interpretations of music, or how to make a mobile. It's interesting. And after four years' association, some of these ideas have rubbed off on me. I notice decoration more than I ever did. I have always been the person who said, 'It can be pretty but it *has* to be useful first.' Slowly but surely I am beginning to see beauty for its own sake. I can't stand poetry quotes but you never can tell, I might even learn to like them, too!

I have not touched the problem of the obvious homosexual. He is in the minority. I think he brings the censure of the public not only on himself, but is the main cause of all adverse judgment against the group as a whole. He is such a rebel and such an exhibitionist that he is held as an example of the homosexual.

I do not welcome this type in the bar. I am rude to them, watch them closely for any infraction of my arbitrary rules, and they soon leave. They refer to me as 'that witch'—not spelled with a 'W.'

They are a menace to my business. If they were welcome, it would not take them long to set the pace for the bar and then I would lose all my preferred customers. I do not know why these blonded limp-wristed boys are so anxious to attract attention. I could guess that it is rebellion against very early restriction at home, but lots of heterosexuals have had close restraint too, so that is not the answer. In one way, being a homosexual is not so much of a problem to them as it is to the more circumspect ones. They have made the decision and feel they have nothing to hide. But of course they are still rebelling or they would not feel the need to show off.

When I first started associating with gay fellows I did not know of the different layers in their social scale. I pulled some dreadful boners. I would invite different ones to my house for Sunday brunch and find to my chagrin that they were not compatible at all. I got dirty looks from each of them. Eventually I learned to be more cautious with my invitations.

Some time ago I promoted a dinner party to go for Spanish food. I told everyone in the bar that if they wanted to go, to be at the bar at seven on Monday, my night off. We piled into cars—25 of us—went for our dinner, and later to some other spots. We had a wonderful time. With that many in the group there was not too much of the caste system showing.

Later I tried it again, this time for a Cantonese dinner. Only nine appeared and it was a flop. There were two distinct groups and although no one was rude, there was no repartee nor jokes and every one was glad to have it over with and leave.

That is my last time for a general invitation. After this I shall hand pick the group or let them do it.

I have been invited to many of their parties. Some of the parties have been very highbrow. An evening of fine music, for instance. Once a whole afternoon of talk by a man who conducts travel tours, with color slides to illustrate.

I have been asked to a scrabble evening or a canasta game and I have the joy of well spent hours.

One thing I can firmly say. Since I have attended these parties I am bored stiff at a party held by straight people. The men get off to one side with their drinks and talk business and the women exchange recipes and talk about Junior's allergy. When I leave this kind of party I wish I had stayed home and read.

As I think about it, maybe their gay problems are not too great after all.

Gay Bar

3

'. . . carry on like Faust . . .'

cannot make an overall statement that all these boys have talent, but the
percentage is very high. At least the results seem to show talent in
artistic fields.

They have one advantage. They can concentrate on the project because
they have solitude. Every pattern of living has its advantages and its shortcomings. In this group lonesomeness is the phantom that hovers over
every one. So they keep active. Add to this a high content of imagination
and capacity for taking pains and we have a good substitute for talent.

A few weeks ago I was asked, with others, to one fellow's home for Sunday dinner. It was my first visit to this apartment and I was surprised to
find that it was in the same building that I once lived in, years ago. In fact
it was the apartment over my former one. I had lived there 15 or 18 years
ago. The building was not new then and you can imagine what time had
done to everything, in spite of the fact that it had excellent upkeep.

When we got inside, I was astonished at the miracle my host had
wrought. His color scheme was black and white. The walls were white and
many pieces of furniture black. Flowers and pictures in color stood out
against this background.

He had taken the crate that comes around a hot water heater, had
painted it black, and had woven two-inch ribbon of the same color

through the frame. It sounds corny, doesn't it? Well it was not. It was a lovely screen converting a difficult corner into a striking work of art, through the simple contrast of textures. A small, old-fashioned lamp stood in front of it on a table.

My ability to describe this is faulty but to me it was charming. I also appreciated it because it was done without much cost. Those who know me will chuckle at this. I am noted in my circle for buying wholesale or at the junk yard.

My host was not much different than the others. They are not hampered by convention in their thinking and this freedom spills over into many fields.

I am thinking of Gil Stone. He wants to write. I think he is just about to click and we are all holding our breath, you might say. He can paint. Does it well too. He is very appreciative of music and has a nice record library.

His art and imagination are a big help to me. He has ideas about decoration in the bar and the one BIG service he does is to make the mobiles that hang in about the center of the room. For almost a year we have tried to have one up on the first day of each month that told the story for the month. Valentines and shamrocks and May baskets. I had to explain these baskets. Not too many knew of the old custom of hanging decorated paper baskets, filled with flowers and candy, on door knobs, ringing the bell and running.

After almost a year of these monthly creations we ran out of ideas and decided to put up one only when the idea strikes us. I say 'us' but I mean Gil.

'I'm getting tired of that and I'm going to make another,' he will say.

All I ask is, 'What supplies do you want me to buy for it?'

He is so clever at using what he has around the house or what I might have at the bar that they rarely cost much.

Sprinkled through the group of people who achieve notable results in any field, there is a small percentage that have a driving talent. But the remainder of this group is made up of persistent and hard-working people who just don't know when to stop. The strange thing is that opportunities present themselves to these people, or perhaps they just recognize the opportunity when it shows. Every once in a while I witness one of these opportunities being seized, many times with fear and trembling, but still seized.

Dan wanted to move. He wanted more space for his hobbies and he wanted to be closer in town. He noticed a 'for rent' sign on a rundown-looking house and called the owner. After some dickering he got it, rent free for a couple of months, while he fixed it up and worked out a deal for low rent after that for services around the yard.

He feels happy in the new place; he's working like a beaver, painting, building shelves, fixing draperies, and the landlord has his property back in good repair. The landlord lives out of town and cannot keep an eye on the place and is glad to have it off his mind.

Many would have passed up the old house as beyond help, but Dan was willing to work and he now has a nice home at low rent.

Lee wanted to discuss a change of jobs with me. I never make any decisions for anyone but sometimes I can come up with some questions that help him decide for himself.

He came in early when business was slow.

'I don't know what to do, Helen. I have a good job now, but I have this chance to start a new department with this new firm.'

'What's holding you back?' I asked. 'Is the money as good as where you are now?'

'Oh, the money is about the same.' He smiled a little. 'The firm is a new concern, but I'm not afraid of that. I just wonder if the job is too big for me. I'd hate to take it and fall down on it. Then I'd be out of the one I have now and that one too.'

'Is it the same type of work that you do now?'

'Yes. I know the work all right. But there is lots of responsibility with the new one.'

He was beginning to show self-confidence now as he talked.

I threw the whole problem right back at him.

'If you are willing to put in long hours and *think* the job for 24 hours a day you can do it.'

41

His face still showed uncertainty, but his walk was firm as he went out the door.

He called me in a few days and told me he had decided to make the change.

A few months later he dropped in again.

'I haven't seen you for ages.' I smiled as I served him his beer.

'Good reason.' His voice was tired. 'I've been on that new job 12 and 14 hours a day, Helen. Boy! Am I tired! I've got it whipped into shape now. I'm head of my department and they seem to like me.'

I was delighted. It showed in my voice as I said, 'I knew you could do it if you wanted to.'

These may not be instances of talent, but they make nice substitutes.

Norman was having a pre-Easter party. The Friday night before. Jim went a little late and did not stay very long. He came in to the bar afterward, chuckling.

'Helen, you know all these stories they tell about gay parties? Orgies! Drinking! Carrying on! You know. Well, I went over to Norman's. You knew he was having a party.'

He stopped to take a sip of beer, then continued.

'I knocked and someone hollered "Come in." I went through the living room to the dining room.

'There were 14 fellows sitting around the big old dining table, *coloring Easter eggs*!'

Jim was laughing now.

'Someone looked up and said, "Hello, Jim," and went back to pasting gold stars on a pink egg. Most of them never looked up. Norman offered to get me a chair and furnish me with some eggs, but you know, Helen, I'm not the Easter egg type. I had to help myself to some beer from the refrigerator. I watched a little bit, looked at a magazine, and came on down here. I knew I'd find some one here to talk to me.'

He left the counter and sat down beside Ken in a booth to tell him about it.

One of the egg painters showed up later with four eggs for me. I placed them on the bar for all to see. They were works of art. Descriptions won't help you see them. They were beautiful—their colors showed against the dark wood of the back bar. They are now in the breakfront at my home.

I have one who comes in who is an illustration of the driving power of real talent. He has not clicked yet but I think he will. As is many times the case, he does not have promotion ability, but he is meeting many people, and in the course of time he will find someone who will take over the business angle for him.

He writes complete revues. The lyrics, the music—some of which is haunting—the dialogue. Two of these shows have been produced by small-town women's clubs, and I think, one of these days, I shall be able to say I knew him when.

He does not have an income so he works at a very menial job in the late afternoon and evening, then he goes home, writes most of the night, and sleeps until it is time to go to work.

I say he comes to my place. He does, but not very often. I won't see him for weeks at a time. But once in a while he gets stale. Then he comes in for a couple of beers and listens to talk. He is not very social. To me, he is a picture of what happens when one is spurred by real talent. For myself, I'll take the substitute of persistent work. It looks like talent, feels like talent. Maybe it would be fair to call it one form of talent.

Possibly this story does not belong in a talent chapter. But it has to be told, and after all, Bill does have a talent, although it is not one he uses in his work. He can make women's hats. He makes his mother's hats and once in a while he makes one for a friend of hers. He is too busy in his work to indulge in this pastime very often, but he has scads of trims on hand, just in case. He loves to do it and he certainly has a flair.

Bill is a very butch character. Heavy voice. Positive manner. His room-mate, Bart, however, is quite the opposite. Not that he is feminine. He is just reserved. He never does anything in public that would attract attention. A very quiet, nice person.

Well it seems they were moving to another apartment. Bill has a convertible and they had it piled high with boxes. Because it was fragile, the box with the hat trimmings was on top.

They were sailing along Sunset Boulevard on a Saturday morning. The traffic was not terribly heavy but there are always cars on this boulevard.

The box full of trimmings flew off, fell open, and plumes and roses and veiling and ribbons scattered *all* over the street.

'Oh, let it go, we can buy more,' begged Bart.

'To hell with that,' Bill said and pulled over to the curb.

Bart started to slide down in the seat and shrink into the corner. Bill got out of the car and, darting and dashing through oncoming traffic, started retrieving the items.

He is a camp at heart and pretty soon he was dancing back to the car holding a plume over his head and a wisp of veiling floating around his shoulders. He worked in and out of the moving cars until he had most of his trimmings, but he had traffic pretty well tied up for a few minutes.

Fortunately no police cars were in the neighborhood. He might have had an awkward time convincing those cops that the trimmings were his own.

Bart was very relieved that he did not see anyone he knew.

THROUGH YEARS OF FRIENDSHIP with gay men, Helen developed great insight into their natures. Her own understanding was inevitably influenced by the popular psychology of the day, but Helen clearly had her own take. This is evident in her remarks on "the boy who is basically homosexual" and her comments about Fred, whom she describes as "a basic homosexual" whose sexual orientation is as immutable as eye color.

Helen's grasp of the "basic," essential nature of homosexuality among the gay men she knew was extraordinary. Having listened to many gay men's accounts of their lives, this woman who discovered a distinctive pattern of characteristics in their hands noted another pattern among them: gender-nonconformity beginning in childhood. "He often enjoys doing the things that are called sissy," Helen states. From a childhood of helping mother with housework, the "basically homosexual" boy—sensitive, neat, polite—often moves into an adolescence of "going around with girls," enjoying their company, affection, and sensibilities, helping them with their choices in clothing and hair styles. "At this stage," Helen says, "a wise adult might detect the tendency toward gay life and by adroit questions and sympathetic talk, help him to face this trait."

Such helpful adults were scarce throughout the country when Helen's boys were growing up. Certainly Harold Call did not encounter one during his childhood and adolescence in rural Missouri through the 1920s and 1930s. "My younger brothers were interested in cowboys and Indian stuff, but I was never interested in that and I was never interested in guns," Hal recalled. "They and Dad were interested in going hunting, shooting rabbits."

Though Hal's memories of growing up offer a narrative of gender-nonconformity different from the "girlfriends" version that Helen describes, they represent another "basically gay" pattern. A National Honor Society member, Hal edited the high school yearbook and newspaper and performed in school plays, sometimes in drag. He enjoyed reading poetry, never dated girls. "When we chose up sides to play a game on the playing field, I was the last one chosen," Hal said. "I was no athlete and I didn't want to be. I wasn't interested in baseball or football; I would play croquet."

Hal Call had a great aversion to gay men's gender-nonconformity, his own and others'. "I never wanted to stand out as the sissy or the gay queen," he said. Serving in the army in World War II, afraid that his buddies would figure him out and ridicule him, Hal told his mother to send him toiletries that were masculine, not "sissified." When Hal met his first lover while stationed in Los Angeles, he liked him because he was educated and sophisticated and "wasn't a flamboyant or sissy looking individual. He looked like any other man and expected the same thing in me." Hal's lover—a homemaking-minded young man who would soon be running his own interior design business in Hollywood—was hardly "like any other man." But like many gay men, including most of Helen's boys, he could act the part convincingly enough.

Hal explained to a fellow Mattachine member, "We accept the fact that the 'fairy' is one of us. Like the blind, the lame and those otherwise handicapped. . . . It may be that they should be exhorted to modify their behavior in public so that they draw less attention and scorn—in fact, we encourage them to do so." Jim Kepner and others felt a surge of confidence when they looked around the auditorium at a 1953 Mattachine convention. "Part of our excitement flowed from our pride that most of us 'didn't look gay,'" Kepner said. "Most of us still expected a crowd of gays to look effeminate and somehow disreputable."

As the American public was beginning to grasp that there were many homosexuals in their midst, and because the public tended to stereotype homosexuals as effeminate fops, issues of self-presentation loomed large for many gay men. Homophile publications of the 1950s are a rich record of what was essentially the first-ever national forum for homosexuals concerning how they wished to see themselves and be seen by others in relation to conventional ideals of manhood.

Donald Webster Cory expressed the prevailing mindset clearly in his landmark book *The Homosexual in America*: "Many homosexuals consider that their greatest fortune, their one saving grace, has been the invisibility of the cross which they have had to bear. The ease with which they were able to hide their temperaments from the closest friends and business associates, from their parents, wives, and children, made it possible to partake

Harold L. "Hal" Call (1917–2000) in 1953, the year he discovered the Mattachine organization at a meeting in Berkeley. Courtesy ONE National Gay and Lesbian Archives.

of the full benefits and material and spiritual advantages life offers to the heterosexual. Many such people—and I include myself—have constantly striven to perfect their technique of concealment."

An earnest, twelve-page essay in *ONE* magazine, "The Margin of Masculinity," detailed how to conduct oneself in a properly masculine way. "First, watch your hands. No other physical factor is such a dead giveaway of the homosexual. . . . Next, Johnnie, learn the upright posture of masculine males. . . . To avoid the danger of ever lolling too prettily, . . . don't ever let the knees or feet touch. It is impossible to strike an overly graceful pose while the legs are spraddled. . . . A miserable trait common to many homosexuals is that of complaining about services received in public—kicking up a fuss over real or fancied slights. . . . When you carry a small package through the streets, never clutch it high on the chest. . . . Skip the gentle expletives, watch your adjectives, and use superlatives sparingly."

The author described observing a man in his early twenties at a gay bar, one of the "blonded limp-wristed" set to which Helen would have given no shelter: "His face could have belonged to any plain and overly self-conscious girl, and when he ordered a draft beer the lyric timbre of his voice did nothing to dispel the illusion. His black leather jacket with its bulky lines would have been out of character had he worn it in the usual manner. Instead, it was thrown around his shoulders in the fashion of a cape—and I knew that sooner or later he would be pulling it close against the ravages of some naughty little draft, after first touching the collar to be sure it stood up in the back. A dark out-cropping at the roots of his fluffy peroxide hair suggested he was slovenly, or maybe just tired of being a blond.

"I have never had any real understanding of this sort of person and there was a day when I detested any semblance to his kind. Now, thank God, I felt a kinship with him. I knew that if the two of us were ever to be accepted by society, the likes of him must first be accepted by the likes of me; accepted without condescension, accepted with the conviction that the only true measure of 'right' behavior and 'wrong' is whether one's actions are harmful to himself or to others. A virile facade wouldn't have changed the weight of this man's mind, the structure of his emotions, or the shape of his soul, and though I would always reserve the right to avoid his type in forming friendships, I knew we were brothers."

But virile facades really mattered in a nation anxious about its men's manliness. A *Mattachine Review* cover highlighting "The Homosexual Swish" asked: "Does he deserve the scorn that society heaps upon him?" An article in *ONE*, "Swish or Swim," lamented the "cowardly-cruel . . . way in which most homophiles seem bent on currying favor with the cultists of hyper-maleness by continually throwing contempt on any who do not wear the present dismal male livery or carry themselves with the tough-guy slouch and so look, sound and smell indistinguishable from the mass."

"Homophiles need to tolerate their own kind," the author insisted. "Everyone who believes in mental health should support the right to non-violent liberty of expression. . . . The homophile that sneers at his fellow homophiles' idiosyncrasies is doing almost the worst service to his own cause and the cause of liberty and the cause of life." The author stated that much mental illness in America results from "the refusal to let people play any but one stiff conventional jejune role."

"Just now American society is in a pretty bad way," a *Mattachine Review* article observed. "We snicker when we see the French general kiss the soldier on both cheeks as he pins the medal on his chest. We don't like another man to embrace us, or put his arm around us—we are the society of the swift firm handshake. Why? What are we really afraid of?"

Readers' letters to *ONE* and the *Mattachine Review* reveal how gay men—that tiny fraction of them who were disposed to read homophile magazines—were reacting to the hyper-conformist culture of the times. Mostly they were making ambitious efforts to blend in. Mr. F. of Ithaca, New York, was succinct in stating the case for conformity: "While some may argue 'why should we hide what we feel compelled to do?' the masking of effeminate traits is essential to the ultimate acceptance of the homosexual by heterosexual society. Besides, most of these 'compulsions' are really one's own desire and will—they can be controlled."

"The flaming faggot who swishes up Lexington Avenue in New York City screaming and calling attention to his eccentricities sets back homosexuality," a New York City gentleman stated. "He is an object of scorn and the general public places all deviates in the same class. He is a menace and decent homos have cause to resent him. I am not frustrated. I do have a sense of humor. I have a responsible position and would lose it immediately were I even suspect."

This reader was also concerned that the magazine was revealing too much of the gay underworld, gay slang in particular: "I cannot go along with you when you present the stupid, frivolous side of homosexuality, feeding material to those who will use it for selfish ends and hold us up to ridicule. I refer to the 'Mary' type of conversation in stories and articles. . . . I know, enjoy and employ the jargon, but never outside the circle. It has its place and that precludes the general public. To give such information in black and white, making it available to scoffers, is a form of suicide. Don't make things more difficult. Let us aim for respect."

"I am a firm believer in homosexual life and think that it is a most beautiful thing," Mr. B. wrote from New York City. "As far as sex goes I too share the opinion that it belongs in private, behind closed doors, and *nowhere else*. The small minority of peephole seekers, toilet queens, screaming faggots and other forms of extremists *must be rooted out at once* to prevent further rumors from spreading. But how? Perhaps those who read *One* and share my opinion can suggest ways."

Mr. D. of Evanston, Illinois, wondered about his fellow gays who insist on being swishy: "I . . . was born with my characteristics and tendencies and NOBODY has had a harder time than have I, but Brothers, we just can't afford to 'swish.'" He found it "not only revolting, but nauseating to those who try to live like MEN, working and living with people. Why should we wear a badge? Why do we insist on using and coining a lot of phraseological jargon which serves to advertise? Why when we attend a cocktail party must we dress in the God-awfullest ostentatious attire that only a queer could assemble? Why do we get so much bang out of John's new 'wife,' or a broken relationship? Is it because we are so shallow and ephemeral that we are only looking for a new thrill?

". . . Ours will be a better world when we as human beings and homos clean up our own doorsteps," Mr. D. declared. "Isn't it much more fun having someone with whom one can talk sensibly, enjoy a dinner out, a concert, or the theater? And whether it goes right or all wrong, isn't the logical, practical thing to do not to talk too much? But maybe it is asking too much for a homo to be logical and practical."

Mr. B.T.S. in Illinois advised the Mattachine Society to offer its members assistance in butching up their self-presentation: "How helpful it would be to say to some of our homosexuals, 'Look, why impede your acceptance with that walk? Come now, square your shoulders and go forward purposefully without moving anything but your arms and legs, like you're going to walk right through a wall. Why louse up your effect on other people with those facial expressions? Here's a mirror. Watch yourself sidewise so you won't be flirting with yourself while you talk. See, put power into your voice.'"

To Mr. D. of Los Angeles, *ONE*'s article "In Defense of Swish" was "a most unfortunate and ill-advised item . . . tragic and dangerous. Not only does this type of driveling philosophy disgust and estrange and thereby cut off the interest and support of the better type of invert who believes inversion can and should be invested with dignity, masculinity and high ideals of conduct and character, but it serves to further prejudice an already dangerously warped concept and attitude of a neurotically biased heterosexual majority toward the homosexual minority."

Mr. P. of Richmond, Virginia, stated, "The public likes nothing better than to hear of a homosexual who is shiftless or irresponsible, or to see a homosexual dressed as a member of the opposite sex and acting like a 'fairy,' at whom they can point with scorn and so dislike all homosexuals." He implored the editor of *ONE* to "show the prejudiced public that the homosexual is not a pervert lurking in dark places, but more often is a decent, hardworking, reliable and often courageous individual who does not inflict his 'differences' on anyone. . . . I am quite sure that so long as we have 'flits' and 'pansies' who want *sympathy*, we will not have tolerance and understanding."

The pansy problem was viewed quite differently by Mr. A. in Brooklyn, New York: "Most normal people are not really offended by the swishes. It is the (to all appearances) normal young man, who is revealed to

51

be gay, that makes them mad. On a certain beach in New York there appears nearly every day a flaming, bleached blonde (it was this season), tall, skinny, outrageous faggot who was the darling of the straight sex. They loved him. And the way he flitted around calling everyone 'honey' and 'love.' It was the gay kids that would gladly, had they got him alone, thrown him in the water and held his head under.

"Would someone please explain to me why I, if I should hold my cigarette the wrong way, or, kidding around, drop my voice and call someone darling, get a dirty look from the 'normals' while a real flame draws only minor chuckles? What do they want us to do, go around with our hair henna'd and our faces made-up, in order that we may conform to their ways of picturing us?"

Don Rifle of Santa Monica fumed about what he saw as an excess of "effeminate," "girlish," "nelly" photos and drawings of males in *ONE*: "I know that many people have a positive predilection for effeminacy, as opposed to true femininity. I don't have such a feeling; in fact an overdose of male girlishness gives me the vapors. . . . Nobody wants *One* to ape the muscle mags with sweaty weightlifters all over the place, but this shouldn't deny us the opportunity of seeing an occasional attractive man in your pages." He stated that "all this grotesquely womanish art is bad psychologically for those of your readers who are battling to free themselves from self-identification with the popularly held homosexual stereotype. Please help them remember once in a while that the average person with homosexual preferences looks, and is, as male as the next guy."

On the other hand, Mr. B. of New York City wanted *ONE* to publish more on transvestism: "I am a man sixty-one years old who has worn feminine attire whenever possible since birth. I am not ashamed of it, in fact I enjoy being seen in one of my many pretty dresses. As I write this I am fully clothed as a lady, from the skin out—nylon stockings and white high-heeled shoes. I also am wearing ear-rings, necklace and bracelets. My friends all admire me and prefer to have me dress as a lady. Perhaps there are many of your readers who dress as I do. Why not let's hear from them?"

A new reader of the *Mattachine Review*, Mr. D.C.S. in California, declared his main pet peeve with society to be the homosexual stereotype:

"A homosexual to 'Mr. Jones' is the hand-on-hip type with distinctive lisp and a yen for public lavatories, etc. If we were to try to find the 'average' American homosexual . . . I sincerely believe he would not be anywhere near the above effeminate model described, but an honest-to-goodness man with but a different cross to bear in life."

"The normal homosexual" found another spokesman in Mr. P. of Hollywood: "There is no reason on God's green earth why a homosexual has to dress differently from other people. If we have good taste, and we all should, we shall want to dress accordingly without regard to who might interest us physically. I believe we are the same as other people most of the way. This sameness, not differentness, should be stressed, both to ourselves and to the outside world."

Rarely appearing in the homophile press were letters from gay men who refused to mask or apologize for their gender-nonconforming traits. Exceptional was Mr. C. of Newburyport, Massachusetts, who wrote, "The homosexual contributes so much of beauty and of mind to our world that I am not ashamed of being one." He reported that he had been unemployed but refused "to lie or make attempts to be a he-man, just to hold a job. I do not mean by this that I am one of those people that go out of their way to wiggle their hips, but I have a soft, cultured voice and a certain effeminate sensitivity that seem to tell people I am 'gay.' I have no intention of submerging my individuality for a lot of weak-kneed conformists who if they were honest with themselves would admit they admire me for having the courage to be a non-conformist, but it is easier for them to join the mob and agree with general condemnations than to stick their necks out."

"I don't claim to have a great deal of courage," Mr. N. wrote from Indianapolis. "I don't make a point of informing everybody of my true feelings. Some people know how I am. Many don't. Neither do I pretend to belong to the over-manly, spit every five seconds, kill the dirty queers group, who are not too good to sneak into back alleys or public rest rooms, or a car on a dark side street."

"Being in the life, I know what it is to be heartbroken, shunned and exploited," said Mr. K. of Philadelphia. "Why there is so much contempt for us I do not know. I have a good job. I have never robbed, murdered, raped or been arrested. I have never used any form of dope or been drunk. I give to the churches and charities, and my sexual life does not include teenagers, nor any form of solicitation on my part. Most of us are the same. The loud obvious type are in the minority, so why are we thought to be such monsters and a menace to society?"

After visiting the Mattachine Society office in San Francisco, one fellow wrote an account of his experience that captured the mix of fear, anxiety, and loathing that informed the lives of many homosexuals: "During my entire adult life (pre-Mattachine), I don't think I've spent one completely relaxed moment in the company of (or even among) other people. Always I've had a little private dragon on my shoulder whispering in my ear: 'Watch it. Act the part. Don't let IT show!'

"We are the furtive. The frightened. And when it comes down to knowledge of homosexuality and homosexuals, we are the unbelievably stupid. . . . We are usually white collar. We are usually married; in sensitive positions, or have some other reasons for our high degree of fear. Usually we became aware of our problem belatedly and have confided in no one.

"We dress well and conservatively. We are positive that no one knows of our problem. (But we are not absolutely certain.) We are certain that we possess none of the give-away traits. (But we are not absolutely positive.) . . .

"Last week I visited your office. And to make that visit I had to summon every bit of courage I possessed. Why? Because of my ignorance and stupidity. I guess I thought I'd find a bunch of impersonator types sitting around, doing needlepoint and chattering in shrill voices. In fact, I guess I thought that (with myself an exception) that is what all homosexuals are.

"What did I find? I met four or five fellows. Friendly, courteous and very nice, intelligent guys. Fellows who look, act and talk like the run-of-the-mill people. Fellows who apparently read, work, relax, worship, eat, drink and live just about the way other citizens—solid and substantial citizens do. And I became aware, for the first time, that the minority group to which I belong is a long way . . . a *long* way *ABOVE* the group I had ignorantly visualized. We are, I suddenly realized, a group for which no apology need be given."

The desire to be seen as "run-of-the-mill people" is central to gay lives from the 1950s to the present. It was a key plank in the Mattachine platform, and Helen made an effort to support it. After remarking that so many of her boys have exceptional artistic imagination and talent coupled with a penchant to be painstaking, she suggests that perhaps it's nothing special in the boys' natures but just the solitude of their daily lives that makes their creativity possible. But one suspects that Helen knew better. She must have known that truly run-of-the-mill men wouldn't have made mobiles for her bar, decorated their homes with creative flair, written revues, made women's hats, or colored Easter eggs—no matter how much solitude they may have faced.

For Hal Call, being a responsible, well-adjusted homosexual meant passing undetected in straight society. Haunted by the stigma of effeminacy, Hal was quick to disparage the idea of homos being different from heteros in any respect other than their sexual inclinations. He had an opportunity to do this during a 1958 radio panel discussion in which he and Blanche Baker participated. When Blanche remarked that "so many homosexuals are very versatile, gifted people," the moderator asked her to say more on the topic. Blanche acknowledged that her observations were not definitive, but that the homosexuals she had come to know were "almost universally . . . the artists, the gifted people, the people who have more versatility and have so much more to give to society. They are not just bread, meat and potatoes people,—they are really talented people."

Though Blanche had been careful to avoid generalizing too broadly, Hal was compelled to correct her. "I know there is . . . the tendency in some of the groups working on the problem today to point out that the homosexual is, possibly, on the average, more gifted than is the non-homosexual," Hal said. "I hardly think this is a just evaluation of the homosexual. I think that he is probably no more gifted on the average than is the ordinary person." He suggested that, to whatever extent gays exhibited unusual talent, it was a result of not marrying and having children, thus having more opportunity to develop creative talents. Blanche did not challenge him on this facile analysis, nor did the moderator, who speculated further that perhaps it was the social hostility and pressure experienced by homosexuals that caused them to make extra efforts to excel.

Soon after making her radio remarks, Blanche clarified to the homophile audience: "I do not claim (as I have often been misquoted) that all homophiles are talented, but I do maintain that like every type of human being they have special things they can do well and I encourage them to make use of any little gift they may have if it is only the ability to cry well. I have had many talented homophiles come to me who are now making good in the world. Yet I am fully aware that there are many criminal, confused and mentally ill homosexuals."

Quite a comedown, but it was what the boys wanted. Grasping the complexities of gay men's circumstances in American life, Helen and Blanche understood that the truth was not always the right answer.

Gay Bar

4

'. . . clever drag, but I think he's fuzz . . .'

T he police play a very important part in my job of running the bar.
There are two parts to the story.

First and most important is the activity of the vice squad. I am more or less in the middle. I realize that in a city of this size, and with the large percentage of inverts here, the police have to have a strong hand in dealing with this situation.

For instance, once or twice every evening, I see a car light come into the parking lot—a high window shows the course of the car—and swing off again. I see a beam of a flashlight as it is sent into the parked cars.

I appreciate this patrol. It keeps down the possibility of patrons leaving the place to sit in the car and carry on. Also it keeps thievery at a minimum. The neighborhood is not of the best, the parking lot is not lighted, and some of the boys have lost articles from their cars. In fact, one fellow complained that someone had tried to pry his radio from the dashboard. That is extreme but it happened. Recently I had a burglary and I talked to the radio patrol. I asked them to keep a close watch and they were very accommodating.

I do have a running battle of wits with members of the vice squad. The police department here says it does not use entrapment. I think this is a matter of semantics.

Young and good looking policemen are dressed as 'gay' as they know how. They are coached in terms of speech and try hard for the mannerisms of the homosexual. They go into a gay bar, act as they think a gay fellow should act and wait for someone to talk to them.

They offer someone a ride or accept a ride and that does it. Some of them play fair, inasmuch as they wait for the gay one to make a pass at them, but many others wait only long enough to get in the car before declaring the arrest. The officer's word, of course, will be taken as true, and they always count on the victim not wanting publicity. They know he will pay the fine and be quiet. The fines for this charge amount to a considerable sum in a year's time. But as I said, this is a large city and lots of money is needed to run it.

I operate the bar alone, and as I do not pay any salaries I do not have to think of the cash register as much as an owner who has to meet a payroll. This is the reason I can be snobbish.

I hand pick my clients. I demand an introduction from one of the regulars before I am cordial to a new patron. Sometimes, if I have been introduced to a newcomer on a very busy night, and if he does not come back very soon, I will forget him. I may not forget his face but I can't identify him so I am cool until he reminds me that he came in with Bob or Bill or Frank.

If I don't know a patron, I give him a warm glass routine. Part of the bar equipment is a large draft beer box and in this is a compartment for chilling glasses. Behind me is a bamboo curtain covering a portion of the back bar shelves. On these shelves is the extra supply of glasses, which are warm, of course. When I serve the stranger, I reach behind me and get him a warm glass. The whole bar buzzes. Those who saw the action tell those who didn't.

A young man sat down at the bar one evening. I stood in front of him to take his order. He spoke in a carrying voice.

'Bert said for you to give me a chilled glass when you give me my beer.'

Those near him, who heard him, looked at me to see how I was going to take this, and when I burst into laughter they did too.

I gave him the cold glass, asked him his first name and introduced him to those near him.

The act of giving the warm glass says 'I don't know this person. No one is to talk to him until I have a chance to find who sent him.'

If someone is so interested that he defies me and talks to him, he, the regular, has bought his last beer in my place.

'If you want to risk your liberty by speaking to someone you don't know,' I tell him, 'you do it somewhere else. You are not going to risk *my* license.'

This sounds melodramatic. It is not. Each arrest made in any bar is reported to the Alcoholic Beverage Control department and a record is kept in the file of the licensee. If neighbors of the bar complain that the place is a nuisance, the police have this record of arrests to substantiate the charge.

My warm glass routine is not to say that I think the stranger is a vice officer. It says only that I do not know this person. However, it forms an excellent barrier to the vice officer since he can't produce a sponsor, nor has he time to sweat it out, or try to find someone who knows him.

The warm glass gives me a chance to check the fellow even if I think he is gay and if others think the same. Many of the gay crowd, knowing that I run such a strict bar, think it is ideal cruising ground because it is safe. I do not tolerate this attitude. It shows up soon and the offender gets the 'heave-ho.' I have a continual struggle keeping the bar a social club. The gratifying part is that my regulars appreciate this so much that they co-operate. They resent anyone who endangers the bar.

This vigilance applies only to the vice squad. I have only appreciation to express to uniformed officers and plainclothesmen.

One of the uniformed officers said to me, 'Helen, we have no prejudices toward you because of the type of bar you run. You pay city taxes and you are entitled to police protection, so do not hesitate calling us if you need us.'

I did that a couple of years ago.

It was the 23rd of December. I remember the date well. Knowing that the next night, Christmas Eve, I was going to be dressed up, I planned to stay and sweep out after I closed. I rarely do this. I always wait until I open the next eve. This is because one of the boys waits for me to go and sees that I get into my car and off the lot safely. I did not want to sweep out the next evening in my 'dress up' clothes. Some of the customers offered to stay but I told them I was not afraid and they left.

At that time I had the theory, since discarded, that if I left the car unlocked, I could walk out quickly, get in the car and lock myself in. I was more afraid of someone lurking around the corner than I was of anyone being in the car. In fact I had not considered that angle at all.

That night I had a cake that had been given to me, a newspaper, my purse and a bag containing the money, and a flashlight. I pulled the bar shut, fastened the padlock and walked the few steps to the car.

As I opened the door, I automatically looked in the back seat. I saw a checkered wool pile on the floor. I thought 'blanket' and then, with a start, I said to myself, 'I don't carry a blanket.'

I closed the car door and walked back to the door of the bar. My hand was shaking like an aspen leaf as I tried to separate the bar keys from the others on the ring. I got the padlock off and as I inserted the door key I looked back and saw a tousled-haired head outlined in the back window.

He saw me look back and after I got in the bar he took off. I reached the phone and dialed the operator.

'Call the police,' I said.

She heard the panic in my voice and asked very quietly, 'What is your number please?'

Believe me, I did not know. The room was dark enough to make it impossible to see it on the phone if I had thought of looking there for it. Finally I said the prefix and the rest of the number came out automatically.

The police telephone operator came on the line just then and I immediately gave him the address before I could forget that too.

I told him I had a man in the back seat of my car. He said very calmly, 'I'll send a couple of the boys right over.'

They were there almost as soon as I reached the front door, but my car was empty then. They searched the lot, asked for a description and we all left.

About a week later, a young man, a stranger, came in, sat on a stool and ordered a beer. I served him and then went to Joe who was sitting at the far end of the counter.

'That's the mackinaw jacket that was in my car last week,' I said.

'Are you sure?' he asked.

'Reasonably, and this fellow's hair is long enough to be tousled as it was last week.'

I came out from behind the counter and walked behind him to step outside for a moment.

When I went back to Joe, he grinned.

'You should have seen his face when you went outside. He did not know whether to go or stay. I think you are right.'

When the suspect had drunk half his beer, I stood in front of him.

'For your information, my car is being locked from now on,' I said.

'I don't know what you mean,' was his answer.

'You know what I mean.' I was very stern.

He gave himself away by his reply.

'You have me confused with someone else.'

I just gave him a dirty look. He took a sip from his glass and left.

The summer after I opened the bar, a 22-year-old toughy sat up front in the corner. He was dirty, wore very tired jeans and a denim jacket. He had not had a haircut for quite a while.

I checked his age, and by some strange chance I remembered his name and address. Usually I am concerned only with the date of birth.

One of my regulars told me that he peddled marijuana around the neighborhood. I could see that he might consider the bar a new hunting ground and I was worried.

I called a police officer, whom I knew, and told him my trouble. He was very helpful.

'Don't try to do anything,' he said. 'A couple of plainclothesmen will be in to see you and you tell them all the details.'

They did come in, took down the name and address of the toughy and some additional information I had been able to garner. I was not troubled any more.

Dope is such a terrible thing that I am a fanatic on the subject. I would cheerfully turn in anyone that I knew was pushing it.

I have had four burglaries in a year. I feel sure it is the same two men each time.

I remember the night they 'cased' the place. They sat at the front end of the counter. It was about one o'clock. They were very quiet and they were not gay. That was apparent. They did not act like trouble makers. No snide remarks to me or to the rest of the bar. They stayed until closing.

As I packed the cold boxes, near them, for the next day, I tried to listen to their conversation but it was so low that I could not hear a word.

Toward closing time, in addition to these two, there were some six or eight regulars in the bar. All sitting in a group at the other end of the counter.

I stood back there with them and in a low voice I warned them.

'These fellows up front are wrong ones. I don't know what they are up to, but when you leave be sure no one is following you. They might try to roll you.'

After I called 'last call' the two left and I did not think any more about them. They were not interested in the customers, that was obvious. But they were interested in how they were going to get in the place.

I will admit they were very nice burglars, as burglars go. They broke open the coin operated machines, leaving no finger prints, closed the side door and did not disturb anything else.

I am on a route. A hamburger stand a few blocks away had breakins the same night each time. I had two further entries last year, timed eight weeks minus a day each time.

The police were extra watchful for a while but after they tired of this close watch it happened again. This is such a widespread city that policing it is a real problem. We do not have foot officers—just patrol cars. There is not as close an association between officer and citizen as in cities smaller in area.

From a percentage standpoint, there are not many homosexuals on the street hunting, but from a numbers standpoint, there are many.

I am aware of this hunting and I do not condone it. I am also aware that it could go on in my bar. But if it starts showing, out goes the offender.

I may be straining at a gnat, but my own boys feel free to bring their mothers, landladies and understanding girl friends, knowing that they will not be embarrassed by someone's actions.

Many members of the homosexual group in this city hate me for my iron hand in a 'not-so-velvet' glove, but some love me and I am happy.

5

'. . . hit him with your beaded bag, May . . .'

In an endeavor to keep the bar a cozy place for my regular customers, I am eternally at war with undesirables. That is, undesirable from our viewpoint.

If an owner of a gay bar does not want the harassment and complaints from the neighbors, he tries to choose a location that is not very elite. In my neighborhood, the large apartment house nearby has police cars standing in front of it many times during the month. The rumor is that some of the girls over there are of easy virtue, and they, of course, do not want to throw stones at me. There are many winos who wander by and occasionally try to wander in. I am not only alert to protect my boys from the ones who want to harm them personally; I am always having to ease out or throw out these neighborhood bums.

I often have girls come in. Singly or in pairs. They may not know the type of place it is, and when they see through the half-opened door a group of well-groomed men, they probably think the picking should be good and they try to come in. Many times they look under age, and are in varying types of dress but I have a stock greeting for them. I lean over the bar before they have had time to ask for a beer, and I say, 'I'm sorry but I do not welcome unattended girls in here.'

Usually they leave without argument. I have had one or two just stand there, looking over the bar, practically drooling. I get tough and say, 'You may go—*now*!'

I can't think of a better place to avoid a husband, if you want to meet another man, than in a homosexual bar.

There have been several such instances since I have operated the bar. The longest lasting was a nurse.

She used to come in with a sandy-haired man, or he would be there waiting for her, once every week or ten days. Sometimes she would be in nurse's uniform, other times in street clothes. She wore a wedding ring and when they came in the first time, I thought they were married and just did not know where they were. They were very quiet, drank three bottles of beer and left before 9:30. Once when she was at the bar first, he came rushing in with a profuse apology. This is not too usual for a husband. I heard her say something to him about her husband and that clued me. As long as they left before my gang came in, I was content.

This meeting went on for weeks and weeks, and as time went on they became more and more familiar. He started putting his hand on her knee or she would lean her head on his shoulder.

One of the regulars said 'You don't let us do that,' and I realized that I was showing favoritism. I walked outside the counter and spoke to them quietly.

'I run this bar for gay fellows. I don't let them do what you are doing, and you can't do it either. Please turn around and face the bar and keep your hands to yourself.'

'Oh I'm sorry,' she said, turning red. 'I did not know.' This was their last time in.

It may seem strange that I would want to run them out since they were not annoying anyone, but their presence put a damper on the conversation. There was never any laughter or wisecracks.

This story will amuse all gay fellows and maybe others as well.

A young fellow came in one night and sat at the front end of the counter. He was in motorcycle clothes. Jeans, leather jacket. All he lacked was the goggles. He was young enough looking to be under age and I checked his selective service card. This check and the warm glass I gave him was a notice to the rest of the bar customers to keep hands off, so to speak.

He started playing the juke box a nickel at a time, going back to his seat each time, and soon one of my regulars, Lee, was there at the juke box with him, picking out numbers.

I sent Gil Stone over to give him the high sign. Lee ignored him. I went to that end of the bar.

'Lee, come here,' I said in a positive voice. He did.

I said, 'I don't know that guy, so you leave him alone.'

'I just want to talk to him, Helen.'

'You let him alone.' I was the school teacher speaking.

He went back to his seat at the bar, but in a few minutes he left and as he went toward the front door I heard his voice, not his words, as he said something to the boy in the leather jacket. Soon he left also and I watched them as they talked outside.

I went back to Gil.

'If you see Lee soon,' I said, 'and want to save him some embarrassment, you better tell him to stay out of here. I'll not only refuse him beer, but I'll give him a piece of my mind as well.'

Gil worked in a large store and as it happened, Lee went in there the next day. Gil told him what I had said.

'She couldn't have seen me,' Lee protested.

'Please, she sees everything,' was Gil's answer.

The sequel to this came early the next week.

The guy in the leather jacket came in shortly before seven. I was not ready to do business and I sent him to a little cafe next door which also had beer.

Fifteen minutes later he came in wanting credit on beer until his friend could get there, but before I could refuse him, another boy in a leather jacket came in with a girl. He bought them both beers under protest. The girl did not want a soft drink and she was too young for beer. She asked where a phone was and I sent her to a booth a short distance away. After she left I stood in front of the boys.

'I'm curious,' I said to the first one. 'Tell me—why did you tell your friend to meet you here?'

'This is classier than the place next door,' he replied.

'I don't mean that. I mean why would you ask him to meet you in a homosexual bar? I thought you boys did not like to be seen coming out of a homosexual bar.'

I let him have the word twice so that he could not miss it.

'I've never been here before,' the new one said very quickly.

'I was here once before, last week,' the first one said.

'I know,' I answered. 'You went away with the little guy in the light colored car.'

'He accosted me outside.'

'Yes, he accosted you outside, and you followed him on your motorcycle. I got the word back the next day that you were *all right*.' I gave the last two words strong emphasis.

His friend gave him a very funny look. They drank their beer in silence and left.

I'll bet the first one had some tall explaining to do.

My place, before I bought it, was referred to as a bucket of blood. It was a hangout of rowdies who staged fist fights on the parking lot hourly on the hour and then came back in to make up with more drinks.

Most of my business neighbors appreciate the peace and quiet that prevail there now. An incident that took place a few years back brought that out.

There is a bar about two blocks away. The owner, a short, chunky man, dislikes me very much. I can't understand this dislike for I am sure he would not want my customers if they went there. Although he may not know it, I send him many people who come in, not knowing where they are, and ask for draft beer.

One Fourth of July he came in with four others. Two sailors who came with them stopped outside when they saw a woman behind the bar.

All those who came in were obviously looking for trouble, but since they did not seem too drunk I thought if I served them one drink they might go.

They lisped and made nasty slurs, trying very hard to get an answer from one of my boys.

They ordered another round.

Instead of serving them I went to the phone and called the police. Then I went back to them and told them I could not let them have any more.

The ringleader, my neighbor, demanded more in a loud voice. When I just stood there, he started throwing ashtrays and tore down some holiday decorations.

'You get out of here right now,' I said, going around the end of the bar.

My stomach had butterflies but my voice was firm.

The ringleader snatched my glasses and threw them on the bar. He pulled back his arm to hit me but one of his buddies grabbed his arm.

'You can't hit a woman,' he said.

They pulled him out, struggling.

This group of seven, including the two sailors who did not come into my place, I found out later had been in two other bars nearby, one of them a gay bar, and one not. They had done damage in each one. The police were late in getting to my place because of calls from these other places. One of the officers, whom I knew, went to the ringleader's place and talked to him. He has not been back.

My other business neighbors, hearing of this attack, were disgusted with him and for the first time showed tolerance of me and the bar.

He still hates me and incites some of his customers into coming in to start trouble. I give them such dirty looks, they usually stay for only one drink and leave.

Then we have the real tourist.

Sometimes it's one couple, more often two couples. The men are the ones who want to see the sights. They have the protection of the wife or girl friend. They feel safe. I have news for them. None of my people would think of talking to them. They park themselves in a booth prepared to sit and laugh at us all. I have an answer for that. After they collect their beer from the counter, warm glasses, of course, I walk along the bar and talk to two or three couples and give them the following instructions:

'One of you turn and look at those in the booth. When you see that they are looking at you, say something to the other, then you both laugh. Say another bit and laugh again.'

After this treatment is repeated several times, our unwelcome guests drink up real fast and go. A bit of laughter follows them and we have the case of the biter being bitten.

I used to have one drunk who came in just to be thrown out. He was quite amusing.

'Watch her throw me out,' he would say, before I could get to the end of the bar.

He was always drunk and I always did throw him out.

He did it for laughs. Once when I went into the little cafe next door, he saw me coming and threw up his arms in an exaggerated gesture of protecting his head. I could not help but be amused at his antics but I maintained my severe school teacher mien.

The worst of these undesirables are the rough characters who get drunk, feel a good fight coming on, and look around for someone to beat up. It is their belief that my customers are sissies and would be easy victims. These 'courageous' guys come in, in groups of three or four spoiling for a fight. They could find one too, except for one thing.

I have a standing order, in capital letters, that no one is to get into a fight in the bar unless I am being attacked and *if* I ask for help. I have had more than one of my boys slide off his stool with fire in his eye, only to have the one next to him grab his arm and say, 'Let Helen handle it. She can do it.'

There is a sound reason for this order of 'no fights.'

If a straight fellow starts a fight and one of my boys gets into it and I have to call the police, the aggressor will always say that my boy made a pass at him and his word will be taken regardless of witnesses. If the belligerent picks on me, an owner, he gets short shrift from the law. *So—no fights.*

I had three characters come in one night. Two I could serve but the third was too drunk. He did not want beer anyway. He wanted a hard drink. The others kept urging him to have a beer.

'Don't push him,' I said. 'I wouldn't serve him anyway. He's too drunk.'

Of course that was the wrong thing to say, as he immediately demanded beer. It looked as if it might be a rough go, but one of my regulars called me from the other end of the bar.

'Helen,' he said, 'there's a police car in front giving a traffic ticket.'

I rushed out the side door, ran to the street and spoke to the officer who was standing by the car.

'Will you stick around for a few minutes? I have a drunk who is belligerent because I won't serve him. I want to see if I can handle him.'

He turned and pointed to the drunk who had just come out the door and was reeling up the street.

'Is that the one?'

I nodded.

'We'd rather handle it,' he said. 'It's more fun that way.' So they wheeled their car and followed him for a block. As I watched they questioned him and then loaded him in the car. When I went back in the bar the other two were quite subdued, finished their drinks and left.

These characters think that since I run a gay bar that I am like an ostrich with my head in the ground and that I think I am fooling everyone. The reverse is true. I am proud of the customers I have.

One more story of these rough ones.

Four of them threw open the front door, leaving it wide open, and swaggered up to the counter. I took the offensive.

'I don't serve loud and raucous people.'

They looked a bit non-plussed, turned and left, leaving the door wide open again. They were noisy as they went to the next bar a block away.

This was one of the evenings when one of my customers was giving me a break by tending bar for a few minutes, so I was out on the floor when the same four came in again, this time very quietly.

I approached one.

'Why do you want to hang around a queer bar?'

We do not use that term for the bar but it is the term they would use.

'You're not talking to me lady,' one of them said.

'I am talking to you. This is a queer bar. You are not a queer. Why do you insist on being in here?'

'We just wanted to buy a beer,' another spoke up. 'Any law against that?'

'There is a law against selling to drunks. You are all drunk and I shall not serve any of you.'

They left quietly.

When I get so bellicose, I am reminded of a bantam hen who will attack anything bothering her chickens. Since I am five feet four, the simile might apply.

One evening, one of my regulars sat in a booth instead of sitting at the counter.

'Why did you sit in the booth?' I asked later. 'You always sit at the counter.'

'When I came in,' he replied, 'I could see that your feathers were all ruffled. I wanted to sit back and see if I could spot the trouble.'

Those who are in often know me well enough to know when something is bothering me. I pace. Up and down, up and down. If I am relaxed, I sit on my stool and they know all is calm and *they* can be relaxed.

One evening I went to the little cafe next door to get a cup of coffee. A customer who was eating his dinner spoke to the owner.

'Hey, Estelle, ain't that that old battle ax that owns the place next door?'

I turned and said very sweetly, 'Yes, I am.'

There are lots of different opinions. Some like me, some don't.

FOR HELEN, HER INCONSPICUOUS TAVERN was a way to make a modest living while improving lives and having fun. "Outrageous they may be to the upholders of morality," Donald Webster Cory and John LeRoy observed of gay bars, "but kept hidden and semi-secret, they hardly seem harmful; in fact, they may be very helpful to the adjustment of some people to their group and to their society."

"I have on several occasions used the Gay Bar as a means of introducing supposedly sympathetic non-homosexuals, as well as extremely introverted homosexuals, into a more liberal view of homosexual life," an editor of *ONE* magazine stated. "For such purposes one naturally uses Gay Bars with a reputation for discretion and well-regulated conduct."

Since the repeal of Prohibition, many gay bars of various sorts had come and gone in Los Angeles by the time Helen opened her bar in 1952. Helen's would be just one tiny twinkle in the city's extensive and ever-changing constellation of gay gathering places. The influx of homosexuals to Los Angeles during and after World War II created a ready market for proprietors willing to accommodate a queer clientele. Whether they flourished or floundered, their establishments eventually gave way to new ones—a succession of taverns from loose to uptight, nightclubs from edgy to elegant, hole-in-the-wall bars with diverse personalities. Among the most popular places in 1950s Hollywood was the House of Ivy. It featured "a Latin organist with a large collection of feathery chapeaux and a repertoire of camp songs including his two special numbers, 'Rose of Washington Square' and 'Second Hand Rose.'"

In downtown L.A., the Crown Jewel, Harold's, and the Waldorf were popular gay bars. Discreet businessmen favored the Crown Jewel because its rules of conduct were strict and one had to present a driver's license to get in, which helped to keep out troublemakers. The popularity of another downtown bar, Maxwell's, was due in part to its proximity to the department stores on Broadway, where many gays worked, and to Pershing Square and the bus stations, where many cruised. Mattachine member Fred Frisbie said that the Maxwell's crowd included "hustlers, drunkards, vice cops, and nellie queens" as well as "reserved gay people." Obviously Maxwell's offered little protection from run-ins with cops or criminals. But as Helen acknowledges, not all gay men desired the kind of closely super-vised bar environment that she enforced with an "iron hand in a 'not-so-velvet' glove."

Helen's was a respectable place where her boys could bring "their mothers, landladies and understanding girl friends" without worrying that they would get an unfavorable impression of the gay world. Keeping out obvious queens and boisterous individuals was central to this effort. Nor would Helen tolerate those who tried to use her bar as a cruising ground. Her boys appreciated Helen's efforts to create a well-regulated gathering place where they were relatively safe from both hostile straights and un-abashed gays.

Considering Helen's attitude in telling her story, it's likely that she gives an accurate account of her success in dealing with Los Angeles police officers and state Alcoholic Beverage Control (ABC) officials. Anticipating that *Gay Bar* would be read by some who were unsympathetic to her cause, she would have chosen her words carefully, but it seems unlikely that she would have omitted significant incidents.

By Helen's account, the police did not raid her bar, the vice squad made no arrests on the premises, she had unremarkable dealings with ABC, and the uniformed officers who patrolled her neighborhood treated her with respect. This was extraordinary. It was attributable in part to the savvy of a mature woman who had lived in Los Angeles for many years, understood gay men quite well, had managed several other gay bars, and was adept in reading people and situations.

In 1951, the year before Helen opened her bar, the California Supreme Court ruled that homosexuals had the right to congregate and be served in any public bar or restaurant. In 1955, a year of major antihomosexual activ-ity throughout the country, the California legislature made it illegal for a bar to serve as a "resort for illegal possessors or users of narcotics, prosti-tutes, pimps, panderers, or sexual perverts." Though this legislation was unconstitutional, it emboldened ABC to suspend or revoke the licenses of gay bars simply as a result of seeing persons they deemed homosexual on the premises. While Helen was writing her book, her bar was an illegal re-sort for perverts. Not until 1959 did a California court case reaffirm "that a license may not be suspended or revoked simply because homosexuals or sexual perverts patronize the bar in question."

Los Angeles police chief William Parker saw homosexuals as a grave danger to society, an element to be suppressed in his fast-growing city. With surveillance by the vice squad and the threat of raids by LAPD and ABC officers, gay bars run by organized crime were often more likely to succeed in managing their relations with law enforcement. Helen seems to have handled things quite well on her own. It helped that hers was a small, low-profile gathering place for a select group of men who made efforts to blend in with the general populace. No screaming-queen drama scenes spilling into the parking lot. Certainly no physical intimacy. Helen's boys understood that their contact with each other in public was limited to handshakes and backslaps, the appropriately masculine mainstays of man-to-man interaction.

"Occasionally, but not frequently, violence breaks out in gay bars," Cory and LeRoy noted, "sometimes as a result of lovers' quarrels, other times as a result of some youth going through an episode of homosexual panic, or perhaps because of the jealousies that grip the gay world." The more gentle nature of many gay males is evident in Helen's observation that her bar is a peaceful place. Before she and her boys moved in, it had been a staging ground for fistfights.

In 1957 a *Hollywood Citizen-News* editorial stated, "The police are alarmed over the presence in Los Angeles of an abnormal percentage of the country's total number of homosexuals. They frequent certain saloon and eating places, parks and streets, creating situations that are obnoxious and alarming to normal people. But legally it is difficult to correct this situation." The newspaper urged Los Angeles to heed the film industry's efforts "to screen their employees and attempt to weed out homosexuals and other abnormal characters. Hordes of abnormal people can do great harm to Los Angeles, just as the presence of even a few obnoxious characters in the film industry can damage it."

Arrests of homosexuals in bars and other public places often escalated just before elections, when incumbent officials wanted to show the public that they were committed to dealing with degenerates. In a letter to *ONE*, a San Francisco gentleman observed, "In one city after another, mayors and police chiefs have made a big fuss about getting rid of all homosexuals because they thought it would please the electorate and draw attention away for their own ineffectualness. This is silly, because the electorate couldn't care less. Even women don't consider homosexuals any real competition. The really vicious Do-Gooders are those who are afraid of their own homosexual impulses."

Snaring homosexuals was a major enterprise for the LAPD. What Helen terms her "running battle of wits" with the vice squad was a battle fought much more intimately by her boys. "Vice cops were to be found all over LA," David Hanna recalled, "in the public lavatories of bus and train stations and department stores, at the YMCA, along Sunset and Hollywood Boulevards in their squad cars, and even along the lovers' lanes of the Hollywood Hills. Out of uniform they would sometimes patrol the bars undercover, and were not easy to identify. They too were young, dressed in suits, white shirts, and ties. They sounded gay, and many of them probably were. But as slight a suggestion as 'How about coming to my place?' was enough for an arrest."

Helen appreciated the vice squad's patrol of her parking lot each evening because it kept things safer and discouraged carryings-on in cars. Apparently Helen's boys escaped the fate of some who parked too near a gay bar, only to learn that vice squad officers had noted their license plate numbers and informed their employers, often leading to job loss. "They were assassinating character at will and causing all kinds of mischief and expense and damage to us as individuals," said Hal Call.

"Going to gay bars, private parties, or being seen with someone who was 'obvious' was much like Russian roulette," Dorr Legg said. Since you couldn't go to a gay bar without subjecting yourself to the police, the cat and mouse routine became a mundane reality for many gays. "Will this be the night that I get busted, beaten up, or blackmailed?" Jim Kepner wondered. Another observed blandly of the bar scene, "One is not surprised or dismayed when police swagger in, usually in pairs, glower menacingly at everybody, hurry back to the men's room to see if anything is going on, glower once more at everybody on their return trip, and swagger out again.

'Vice,' quite likely, in a sharp turtle-neck sweater, is ogling you from your very elbow."

Big-city law enforcement departments across the country used undercover officers to snare homosexuals, as did the California ABC. In Los Angeles the police department and the ABC were able to recruit from among the many handsome young men who needed jobs while they aspired to movie careers. Their good looks and acting abilities often proved disastrous for men who responded to their attentions. Vice officers were always believed over the accused and were known to give false testimony to bolster their position. "Improper touching." "Offer to provide sexual services." "Solicitation of sexual services." Being convicted of lewd and lascivious conduct, the most common charge against those who were arrested by vice officers, meant being registered as a sex offender for life. Thus did many men disintegrate into depression, alcoholism, and suicide.

Soliciting or engaging in homosexual activity was illegal, but the intensity of antihomosexual sentiment in American culture led many gays to assume mistakenly that just being homosexual was a crime. In addition, gay men were often ignorant of their legal rights and police officers were not required to inform arrested persons of their rights. As a result, many men who had done nothing illegal would plead guilty, pay the fine, and wind up with a record.

In 1952 Los Angeles resident Dale Jennings elected not to go along with this tradition. In jail after being aggressively entrapped by a "big, rough looking character" who was said to have followed him home uninvited and forced his way in, Jennings was visited the next morning by fellow Mattachine member Harry Hay, who posted bail for him. Hay convinced Jennings to go to court and declare that he was indeed homosexual but not guilty as charged. When the jury agreed with Jennings's attorney—that Jennings acted in a neither "lewd" nor "dissolute" manner and that the arresting officer was "the only pervert in this courtroom"—Dale Jennings became America's first poster boy for homosexual freedom. As word of this victory spread around the country, contributions "to help eliminate gangster methods by the police" flowed to Mattachine's anti-entrapment committee.

In Hal Call's view, "The cops could do any damn thing they wanted. All we could do was run and hide." Though he was highly sexual and craved variety, Hal was not one to cruise public men's rooms. It was caution born of experience. Hal's arrest in Chicago in 1952 had cost him his job, his professional reputation, and a large sum of money. "It was too dangerous," he said of the tearoom trade. "Cops would stand there with a hard-on and look at you. When you made a move on them, they'd arrest you. They called it 'enticement;' we called it 'entrapment.' But, the officers were given quotas *and* they'd rather arrest a queer with a hard-on showing than look down the barrel of a revolver."

Considering Helen's remark that "this is a large city and lots of money is needed to run it," and Hal's statement that vice officers were given arrest quotas, one might reasonably wonder which group of authorities—psychoanalysts or police officers—extracted more revenue from homosexuals. Also looking for their fee, which often amounted to a year's pay, were lawyers—the few who were willing to help homosexual clients.

Hal Call was characteristically blunt in explaining why the police played cat and mouse with gay men but not lesbians: "The male homosexual, because he was a cocksucker and because he played with his penis and somebody else's penis, was a threat to the straight man. That's where the whole problem was." A lesbian stated things equally plainly: "The boys are so horny. They just can't wait." Mattachine's major focus on fighting police entrapment did not inspire lesbians to join the organization. One woman recalled "a lot of animosity and resentment over the fact it was the gay guys who were creating such havoc with the police—the raids, the indiscriminate sex, their bathroom habits, and everything else." Another lesbian left the group, in part because she was unable to reconcile gay men's sexual practices with the Mattachine idea that homosexuals "are people like other people."

The Mattachine Society never had more than a few hundred members nationwide. Many potential members were afraid to be associated with a homophile organization. Another impediment to membership growth was expressed by Mr. E.D. in Ohio as he dithered about whether or not to renew: "As much as I'm ashamed to admit it, I'm afraid my own grand passion is not for social reform (though I ardently desire it) but for homosexuals themselves." This was a sentiment with which the men of Mattachine were very familiar. "Why should I join your organization or subscribe to your magazine?" a dapper gentleman said brightly to a dismayed Mattachine figure in a cartoon in the *Review*. "I'm not interested in your suggestions, and besides my landlady might find out my name is on your mailing list."

It really rankled Hal Call that the organization's membership was always small. "Homosexuals, as a group, are neurotic—believe us," he told a fellow Mattachine. "We have met thousands of them over the past several years. By and large they couldn't care less about our project, our magazine, or anything we are trying to do. . . . But, when they run afoul of the law, the song—and chorus—is changed. Then they want to help. . . . Can you find a better description of a manifestation of neurosis? I think not!"

Hal's sentiments echoed those of Henry Gerber, whose pioneering efforts on behalf of homosexual rights were squashed by Chicago police in 1925. Some years later, Gerber sniffed at another fellow's plan to produce an enlightening publication for homophiles: "If a pamphlet for the initiated it would be a commercial failure from the start for the wicked never like to part from their pennies. It all goes for K.Y."

Gay Bar

6

'. . . meanwhile, back at the palace . . .'

When these boys join forces and set up housekeeping, they are said to be married. They refer to each other as roommates and they behave similar to a heterosexually married couple.

Many people have the idea that one is masculine and the other feminine but this is not often true, at least from what I have been able to observe. They both work. Each may assume certain duties in the house according to his particular talents. One may be a better cook than the other, but believe me, they both can cook. One may supervise the decorating but they both wield the paint brush. They share the expenses of the house. Possibly one assumes the task of food shopping, but this depends on who has the car and the time for it.

Our bar has a club atmosphere, therefore many alliances are started in the bar. The result is always the same. I lose a customer or rather I lose two. Not for good, but they are not in so often.

One of the boys said to me, 'Who is the one sitting the fourth from the end? Do you know him?'

'Oh yes,' I replied, 'He comes in a couple of times a week after night school.'

'How is it I haven't seen him before?'

'Well, he doesn't stay long as a rule, and you usually come in after 10:30, so your paths don't cross. Do you want to meet him?'

'Yes, but wait until it isn't noticeable.'

'Then go and play the juke box, sit on the stool next to him. Listen to the words of the record, and I'll introduce you.'

He followed my directions and in a short while I wandered that way, stopped and said, 'Frank, do you know Ray?' A new romance was on its way.

Those two were soon in deep conversation, comparing their preferences in music, discussing the latest play, exchanging recipes, offering to get a shirt at a discount and showing all the symptoms of a deep new interest. Soon Frank, who goes to night school and has to get up early for work, said he had to leave and promised to be in Thursday after class.

When he left, Ray was beaming. He thought Frank was terrific. He thanked me ardently for making it possible for them to meet and told me they had a date in the bar on Thursday. He wanted me to say that I think Frank liked him, wanted my assurance that Frank would keep his date.

Sometimes there are many meetings in the bar, when these new interests start. They learn to know each other well before taking the step of renting an apartment together. When this is true, I feel sure that if and when they do start living together, it will probably last a long time.

Others are impulsive, and after a few days of seeing each other as often and as long as possible, they move together.

Long time or short time, this 'learning to love you' bit always ends in one story for me. I don't see them except for a short visit on Saturday night. Knowing how lonesome each of them has been I am happy that they are together.

One of a pair of roommates will come in and sit alone at the end of the bar. He stares into his beer.

When I have served him I say casually, 'Curt working?'

This question will open the flood gates and I hear one side of a story. Maybe it will be a complaint of domination caused by jealousy, or infidelity proved by the fact that Curt did not come home last night or just a plain fight.

I hear it all. I try to be non-committal but if the one who is talking to me is unreasonable, I don't pull any punches. I tell him he is acting silly and that he better go home and say he is sorry.

What I am trying to bring out is that the home life and loves of my boys is not much different than the home life and loves of heterosexuals.

I can think of many couples who have met and joined forces since I have known them, and are really making headway in their careers.

Robin and Ike, for instance. They bought a ten-unit rental dwelling shortly after they went together. They have turned back all the rentals toward payments on the building and have it nearly paid for. Each one has kept his job, well paid ones, incidentally, and the last time they came in was to show me a new car Robin had bought, for cash. Ike had bought his a few months back.

Ken and Jack started their home life about three years ago.

They now own their own furniture, a new car, and each is expressing himself in an artistic line as a hobby.

Another couple I know own a house in the valley and the mother of one of them lives with them. Their home is a decorator's dream and they give fabulous parties. These two have lived together for nine years.

As in the case in heterosexual marriages, not all the unions are successful. I am thinking of Jimmie. He is generous to a fault. He has an income in addition to a very sizeable salary. He became interested in Brian who was rather shy, or seemed so, but I knew from reliable sources that the boys considered him a gold digger.

When Jimmie became so enthusiastic about Brian, I tried to get him to take it easy. But he had found someone that would accept his affection and everything else he could offer; he was beyond listening.

'The word unasked for returns unheard,' a wise man once told me. I try to keep this axiom in mind. I gave up trying to slow Jimmie down to a walk and just watched.

81

Jimmie and Brian set up housekeeping and we did not see them for some time. Months later Jimmie came in.

'You tried to tell me, didn't you?'

I played it thick-skulled.

'Tried to tell you what?'

'You tried to tell me he was a gold digger, didn't you?'

'Probably. Well, is he?'

'He sure is. I told him my extra income had been shut off, and that did it. He told me he had never loved me anyhow, so I moved out.'

That ended another romance.

Helen states that among homosexuals "lonesomeness is the phantom that hovers over every one." The author of a *ONE* magazine article on gay bars concurred: "Among homosexuals the feeling of isolation is exceptionally prevalent and often cruel." Both Helen and Blanche remark repeatedly on the dejected longing for companionship, the dark well of loneliness. Through the years, each of them had heard many tales of desperate isolation.

Mattachine and ONE were often overwhelmed with letters from isolated individuals around the country looking for information, encouragement, support, or just a chance to express themselves candidly to an understanding stranger. "There is much persecution, suffering and loneliness in our so-called 'land of the free,'" a gentleman wrote from Michigan. A *ONE* reader in Sun Valley, California, wrote, "Seeing your outstanding example gave me the strength and urge to come out of the isolation and loneliness in which I had buried myself for so many years."

"If anyone would know just how badly I need the affection of someone, and of my own gender, it would naturally be you people at ONE," wrote an Ohio college student in his early twenties. "We so-called 'gay' people are a lonely race; our satisfactions are generally brief and are not long-lasting. A forlorn wandering is our fate. And we are doomed to our emotions which encounter so much difficulty and frustration in being satisfied. I have wished . . . that there did or could exist a 'gay' equivalent to the lonely-hearts clubs found in various papers and magazines. For who is more lonely than most gay individuals? But I realize that such a service or organization is likely to be illegal. Maybe you can offer some practical advice on how I might go about finding myself a soul-mate? I know about the gay bars but I am not one for bars or one night stands. One of the best ways of getting to know persons I think is through writing. So it is that I wish I had someone to write to. As it is, I am bunched up into a ball of misery and don't know anyone."

Correspondence clubs had long facilitated discreet pen-pal connections among gay men. The editors of the *Mattachine Review* and ONE heard from many readers who hoped they would do the same. "I have taken interest in a letter appearing in the December issue from 'Ronnie,'" a *Mattachine* reader wrote. "Like him, I am 18 years old and want to help in any way I can. I realize the Society's position concerning age and participation in organization work, however I would appreciate 'Ronnie's' address. I feel we would no doubt find much in common."

Mattachine, like ONE, required that members be at least twenty-one, and was adamant in its refusals to facilitate contacts. "Sorry, but the request cannot be granted," editor Hal Call replied. "Postal laws would be invoked if the *Review* or the Society ever engaged in any such exchange of addresses. The rule, therefore, is inviolable."

"I am 26, very lonely and disgusted," Mr. E. wrote to *ONE* from New Albany, Indiana. "I'm alone, can't seem to find anyone to care for me or care what I feel. I've written this to you to ask if you can offer me advice. Please forgive me if I've taken up your time for what may seem unimportant to most people. But I'm really most sincere. A friend used to send me quite a few copies of ONE. It makes me feel good to know that there are places where one can live and be happy."

The editor's weary reply was well-worn: "You can easily understand that from among the many thousands of readers we frequently receive such letters as yours. There are many localities and circumstances where the going is not easy. The most our little staff can possibly undertake at present is to publish ONE Magazine, as something of an encouragement and rallying focus for the scattered thousands in all parts of the world. This keeps us busy night and day. There are many questions you alone can answer for yourself. In the long run, rough though it may now seem, you will find yourself the stronger for these struggles."

Mr. B. of Hartford, Connecticut, offered a more sympathetic reply to Mr. E.'s appeal: "I'm in my early twenties and often find life depressing and lonely. I understand how hard it is to accept this, but who knows what will happen in the future? There is always a future. I do hope this note will be of some small comfort. You aren't alone when it comes to feeling loneliness. There are hundreds of us in the same predicament. Keeping busy is a help."

Enlisting psychiatrist Blanche Baker as advice columnist relieved the *ONE* staff of some correspondence burden. Prime material for the column came in letters expressing common concerns such as loneliness and the search for loving companionship.

"I have been receiving ONE Magazine for the past two years," wrote B.C. "I've found ONE to be a friend and a comfort each month.

"Since my discovery of gay life I've found the life to be extremely lonesome and difficult. During the two years of discovering myself, life has been disappointing. The only consolation I have is some day to find happiness and the love of another.

"I also have the problem of my parents. My family is forever questioning my future plans concerning marriage. I know that marriage as others think of it is out of the question for me. I have seen others in the homosexual life attempt it and break the hearts of all involved.

"What is there to youth if I can't find some happiness from loving and being loved in return. Oh! Yes there are such romances if you want to call them that, where the people go together for a few weeks and then look for another. Sex isn't everything; if love is only sex then I don't want it. To me, love is two people living as one and sex is the highest goal of love. It expresses beauty and joy.

"I don't want a Greek God; I want someone who will love me as I will love him, with whom it is possible to be sincere, with whom I have something in common, and with whom I can enjoy the simple things of life—a relationship in which we can find a home and live together. I guess many of us have these dreams which will never be fulfilled. Today we are young and before we realize it tomorrow is upon us with middleage and the same lonesomeness as in youth.

"It is too bad there is not someone each of us can find as life partners. It seems that at least half of us are afraid of the world because we are not accepted in society. We are afraid to lose our jobs and futures. Let us hope future generations will find matters easier. We may not see the day that homosexuals are accepted, but we can try to make it easier for others so they won't have the many problems that we have at the present time."

Blanche answered that B.C.'s letter "touches one of the commonest complaints of homophiles—that of loneliness. Yet this is not the unique problem of homophiles alone. In the bisexual and heterosexual realms there is a host of old maids, bachelors and even many married people who suffer from a profound sense of loneliness, isolation and lack of soul satisfying companionship. This condition seems to be associated with a sense of being different. It may be the price we must pay if we are to go higher up the scale of human evolution emerging from the state of being a herd animal and becoming aware of one's self as a unique creature—one who dares to walk alone.

"Since homophiles are generally considered to be 'different' it is to be expected that they will feel a sense of separateness. It seems to me there is just no answer to the problem other than going deep into one's own self awareness seeking for self understanding and self acceptance. I have known supreme loneliness at times and the only answer I have found is that by accepting myself, with all my own peculiarities and quirks, I have felt more at peace with myself and lo!—there I found others all around me who had walked the lonely road and were delighted to find another human being had had experiences similar to their own and could speak their own language. There may be people all around us who would make delightful companions but if we are so involved in our own self concern or are trying so hard to find the 'right' one, we pass him by in our over zealous pursuit of our 'ideal.' When we can begin to take ourselves less seriously, it is surprising how many we run into who have had similar experiences to our own. Perhaps we aren't as unique as we think we are!"

This exchange elicited a letter from J.H.D., who wrote of himself in the third person: "This correspondent (like B.C.) has known the anguish of loneliness and can sympathise with anyone who has undergone the torture of it. At least B.C. is still a young man with his life ahead of him during which time he may have the opportunity to form the friendship with a member of his own type. This correspondent has not been so fortunate. He is now in his middle fifties without the knowledge of how to go about meeting gay fellows like himself. . . .

"This correspondent has been classified by psychiatrists as heterosexual in past years—he had four nervous breakdowns within the past twelve years as belonging in the latter category. He himself feels that he has always been a homosexual no matter what the medical authorities may have stated to the contrary. This correspondent has known that fact since his early teens. He unfortunately married early as advised by his family doctor as a means of getting over the difficulty of leading a homosexual life on the inactive side. He could not possibly have done anything worse. He had known loneliness before that marriage but it was nothing compared to the terrible loneliness of what it was during the past thirty years of married life. No doubt the suppression that went into trying to live like a heterosexual has much to do with his past four so-called nervous breakdowns. My advice to B.C., if I may make it, would be to try to be patient and to try if he can to form friendships with his own kind. He is, I believe, absolutely right in deciding not to ever marry any woman. Such marriages only bring grief to both parties and certainly cannot bring much, if any, happiness."

Letters from lonesome homosexuals did not always inspire sympathetic responses in readers. "I am a very happy, well-adjusted 'old aunty' because I learned years ago that when I can't have what I want I enjoy what I can get," said Mr. B. of San Francisco. "I don't want to chisel in on Dr. Baker's department, but I wish you would tell those pour souls who moan about being lonely to just quit being so damn selfish. Instead of sitting around feeling so sorry because Prince (or Princess) Charming doesn't discover them, tell them to get out and be friendly with everyone with whom they come in contact. They will be surprised how many of them will respond."

"I am no youngster and from my experiences, and God knows I have had many of them, I will always say no one ever is alone!" said another San Franciscan, Mr. L. "These fruity bastards who complain about loneliness are nothing but conceited bitches who must invariably have an audience to show off for."

Helen states that she is acquainted with "many couples who have met and joined forces" since she has known them, and her bar played an important part in launching some of those alliances. Helen's scant treatment of gay marriages may reflect the fact that most of her boys were unattached and looked to Helen and her bar for companionship to a degree that couples did not. Further, Helen's own experience of marriage was spotty. Her first marriage, compromised by incompatibility and her husband's alcoholism, ended after fifteen years, when Zeb found another woman. Helen's two subsequent forays into marriage were short-lived. Like some of her boys, she seems to have discovered that she was best suited to singlehood despite the inevitable lonely times.

An exceptional letter to columnist Blanche Baker from C.L.R. of Bakersfield, California, presented "some data on the less ephemeral type of gay marriage." Earnest, opinionated, and insightful, it provides a view of gay marriage in the 1950s to complement Helen's remarks.

"I have been a partner in a gay marriage for the last eight years. Our relationship is based upon love, and what is equally important, similar interests and abilities. This latter fact has doubtless contributed to the lasting relationship, although it was not planned this way. Love came first. I met my friend while on a 30 day leave from the army and we had a wonderful month together. After I returned from Korea, we set up housekeeping with my mother while I finished my university work and then moved out on our own. Of course my mother had to know of our relationship. While I cannot say that she was delighted, she was not outwardly antagonistic. Currently, due to my mother's advanced age, we are again living under the same roof.

"We are both university graduates and professional people, although in entirely different fields. We have many things in common but are far from being Tweedle-dum and Tweedle-dee. We believe in and practice sexual fidelity and consider it a necessary stone in the foundation of any such permanent relationship. We have our ups and downs but share an underlying conviction of permanence in our relationship.

"Circulating to some extent in the gay world, I have the opportunity to observe many homosexuals, of both the single and married variety. I must confess that I know few happily married homosexuals, but that is not to say that I know of no such relationships. It will be obvious that gay marriages have many strikes against them from the start, which range from the reluctance on the part of landladies to rent to two single men to the lack of legal and parental compulsion in the direction of permanence. Gay marriages, therefore, seem to be of a temporary nature in most instances. They are frequently mere infatuations, or if potentially lasting love is involved it is often one-sided. Also we must recognize the numerous opportunities and temptations toward infidelity which destroy both gay and heterosexual marriages but which find the homosexual marriage more vulnerable. Few people realize how easy it is for a homosexual to have extracurricular affairs. Not only are there numerous other homosexuals available, but heterosexually married men can be found in large numbers in any city who are not in the least opposed to homosexual contacts. This gives rise to the saying that 'all men are gay until proved otherwise.'

"Lasting gay marriages would appear to fall into two categories. First, there is the marriage of convenience. This marriage may contain an element of true affection on both sides or it may be that only one of the partners is in love with the other.

"Few gay marriages of convenience last any length of time but of course there are exceptions to any rule. These marriages are held together by one-sided love, financial dependence or the enjoyment of a nice apartment which would be denied to both partners were they to live single lives. These fellows are sometimes called 'married sisters,' indicating their superficial nature. This type of relationship is frequently the end result of a marriage which started out as a genuine affair of mutual love.

"The other broad category is that of a genuine love-bound marriage. This is as idealized by homosexuals as it is by heterosexuals. This type of relationship is the avowed goal of many single homosexuals but closer observations reveal that such will probably never come to pass for most of them because either they are incapable of the degrees of unselfishness required or are really having a ball as a single queen and are merely blowing off steam when they express such desires. There is only the question of old age which gives such homosexuals pause in their wild promiscuity.

"I am inclined to feel that the permanent homosexual marriage has been somewhat slighted by not only One Magazine (perhaps their staff members are all single and cynical) but by psychologists and others interested in human relationships and personal adjustment. Possibly this is due to the fact that many married homosexuals view the mad world of the single queen as both dangerous and amusing and are reluctant to make themselves known, preferring to confine their social life to a small group of similarly adjusted people. Also, the married homosexual who includes many single gay men in his social sphere runs the risk of jeers and derision on the subject of sexual fidelity and this often contributes nothing to their permanent relationship. Additionally, we must recognize that single and married homosexuals have few things in common. The single queens talk on and on about the tricks they've had or nearly had and the married team is more interested in the chair they've just reupholstered, the new set of silver that their savings have enabled them to buy or other terribly boring household or common experiences with which the single queen has no patience.

"One can go on to great lengths on the subject of what might have been. If society's view of homosexuals was more tolerant; if the law was less one-sided; if employers were more understanding, would then the homosexual marriage be more prevalent and more desirable? It may be so. If the Department of Internal Revenue allowed married homosexuals the right to file a joint return, things might be much improved also. Homosexuals are easily led into the trap of blaming the social order and attitude for their plight. In the final analysis the gay marriage must be based on a belief in the institution as such, on mutual love, common interests and abilities and upon self discipline. Age is also a major consideration. Many homosexuals cut a ridiculous figure in chasing after chicken and few sights are sadder than the middle-aged or old homosexual who is keeping a young lover for in most cases the end is easily predictable.

"I will now recount some facts about the relationship between my partner and I which you might possibly find interesting. We are both in our early thirties. We have been together since 1952. I had one or two satisfying homosexual experiences in my adolescence but did not enter gay life completely until I married my partner. During my adolescence I was aware of my homosexual inclinations but dated girls in the belief that I might grow out of these desires. My partner realized his homosexual leaning in his early childhood and was a thoroughgoing homosexual when I met him. Parents on both sides know the score and I am accepted in his home by his parents when we make a rare visit there. We have a joint bank account and none of the furniture belongs to either one of us as such.

"We do not have a social life apart from one another except as our jobs demand, which is not often. We socialize mainly with other married couples who share our interests and type of marriage. We know about three 'genuine' gay marriages among male homosexuals, numerous marriages of varying degrees of convenience and two or three marriages among Lesbians. . . . Many of our friends from back east have preceded us to this state, so making friends is no great problem. Perhaps I should say making acquaintances instead of friends, but we count ourselves fortunate to know several couples quite well and we call them friends with more than average correctness. We also know several homosexuals who maintain a heterosexual marriage, the aspect of which provides varying degrees of amusement and pathos."

Blanche thanked C.L.R. of Bakersfield for his "sane appraisal of the adjusted homosexual partnership." She stated, "It has been claimed that a homosexual marriage is bound to be unsuccessful because homophiles are said to be 'unstable, neurotic and promiscuous individuals.' I do not deny that many homosexual individuals may thus be described, but I do not find that these negative qualities are always associated with homosexuals per se. I find that these negative qualities are quite frequently associated with heterosexual individuals as well. As a matter of fact, maladjusted homosexuals closely resemble female prostitutes in these negative aspects. The basic cause behind instability, neuroticism and promiscuity seems to be lack of self-confidence and appreciation of one's self as an individual. Such a person is keenly aware of social disapproval, especially in the sexual realm, which enhances his self-destructive or masochistic tendencies.

"The homo- and bi-sexual individuals are natural variants of the human species, the products of hereditary variations combined with early environmental factors, especially the attitudes of father and mother. Since such individuals tend to feel that they are different from other children quite early in life they are sensitive especially to negative criticism and tend to develop the negative qualities we are discussing. However, there are homo- and bi-sexual individuals who are more fortunate in their early environment where their differences were accepted and not criticized or condemned; thus they mature more successfully, becoming adjusted individuals who live quiet, creative lives in their own unique way and never need to find the path to the psychiatrist's office. I count quite a number of such individuals among my friends; and I suspect that there would be a great many more such useful members of society if homosexuality were more widely understood and accepted. I would like to see children who show homosexual tendencies early in life given a more unique type of education so that they can better understand and accept themselves. Then they would be more capable of forming and maintaining the close creative relationships with their own kind which have been referred to as the 'gay' or 'homo' marriage. As you have indicated, the more successful marriage is based on friendship and common interest, rather than on 'cruising' and one-night stands."

Blanche concluded, "Let us create an ideal of success in homosexual relationships. We have been hearing all too much about the unhappy failures who need these letters to strengthen their efforts towards happiness."

7

'. . . and away we go . . .'

Over and over I have been asked how I got started with gay fellows. It
has been a gradual convergence.

For many years I worked in night clubs as a character analyst,
using my knowledge of palmistry as an entertainment feature. It was there
that I became aware that some of the men entertainers were different, but
being unsophisticated, it took me a while to realize that they were homosexuals. Even then I did not fully understand the situation. I enjoyed being
with them. They were always interesting and amusing.

At that time I met Von. He had a large house that he was operating as a
guest house. His paying guests were all gay but no mention was made of it,
of course. I had dinner there one evening and met them all. The dinner
table was beautifully appointed and the dinner was scrumptious. If laughter and cheer aid digestion, they should all have been the picture of health.

After that I saw him frequently for a time. He came to some of my
gatherings and was the life of the party. Several years passed and I saw him
less often. Once in a while he came to the restaurant in which I was entertaining and I sat and talked with him while he ate. Once he told me he was
a host in a night club and I went there to see him.

The place was filled with men only, good looking, well groomed and
soft spoken. He said something about it being a gay spot, but I was not
interested as I had found someone I knew and was talking to him.

After I was home, I thought about all those men as a group. I wondered if there would be any characteristics that would be prevalent in their hands. I wanted to research for my own satisfaction.

I talked to Von and he talked to the owner of the club. The result was that I went there two times a week, left cards on the tables telling my beliefs in palmistry and talking to those interested in this science. I got paid in tips. I did find a pattern of characteristics visible in almost every hand. Today I use that knowledge in judging a new customer in the bar.

Later Von, discovering that I could cook, said that we should start an eating place. We tossed ideas back and forth for a while. A friend of mine owned a large old house. It had been recently vacated and was difficult to rent. Von rented it and renovated it. He decorated it tastefully with a minimum of expense. He rented the rooms to gay fellows.

Von and I had a verbal agreement. I was to live in the house, acting as house mother. We would serve an evening meal which I would cook. Guests for dinner came by appointment only. They called before 1:30 and I put their name in the pot. I was to draw an expense account of $50 and after we had paid off the initial costs we were to split the profits. It took a while to get rolling. Eventually we had from 25 to 35 guests each evening.

I shall never forget those dinners. Von is one of the wittiest persons I have ever known. He kept the guests in stitches all through the meal.

I had some help in serving and dishwashing. Many times some of the guests would pitch in and help with the cleaning up process.

The living room of this house was 40 feet long. Many evenings it was cluttered with card tables. Canasta was the favorite, although there were some bridge addicts in the house. We sat up until all hours. Someone might go for beer and once we popped corn in the open fireplace. Only once. It was a job. We got red faces and poorly popped corn and after that we popped it in the kitchen.

Five months after we started the food project I told Von that the next month we could start splitting the profits.

'What split?' he asked.

'Half of the profits, as we agreed,' I answered.

'That split was for parties only.'

His answer stunned me. We had not had any parties. I did not argue. I started packing, told him I was leaving and went.

Some months later I met a bartender who was planning a change in a bar. It was to be changed to a gay bar. He knew I had a large circle of gay friends and he offered me a job as hostess. I compiled a large mailing list, with the help of my friends, and we made the change over to a gay bar.

That place folded shortly, but through a boy who came there, I met a straight man, a bar owner, who wanted to change his place to a gay bar.

I took over.

I stayed in this bar for several months and became quite experienced in operating a gay bar. Later he fired me in order to bring in someone else. This new host had a reputation for a following and the boss thought to hold my group and acquire his. It did not work that way. Many of my friends followed me and the new fellow was fired after a month.

I approached another bar owner who, the grapevine reported, wanted to have gay customers. He was glad to have me work there. I opened there in a few days. We had a large opening. After a time I could see that I could not hold them there. The owners of all these places that I changed to gay bars were straight men and had no real understanding of my boys. They were interested in the ring of the cash register and this atmosphere was not hospitable nor attractive.

I conceived the idea while I was there that I wanted my own place so that I could run it my own way. I did not want to be in the middle between the grasping owner and my friends.

I started on a shoestring, borrowed money at that!

At first I had to order beer twice a week. I did not have enough money to get a week's supply at a time. It took about three months to get rolling and after that I began to pull out of the red.

I have never made large sums of money. I am too particular in choosing my customers. Thinking in terms of large money takes lots of energy and I realize my limitations.

Gay Bar

8

'. . . must be these high heels I'm wearing . . .'

Speaking selfishly, probably the outstanding fascination in operating the bar is the fun we have. There is never a dull moment. The fast repartee goes over my head at times and they get a laugh at my puzzled expression. If I chuckle a bit later, that brings another laugh at my slowness. There is no maliciousness in the laughter, just fondness for me even if I am slow. I have a feeling of being in my home and they are my guests.

'Anyone for popcorn?' I'll ask occasionally.

'You know you are going to pop some,' Bill will say. 'So why blame it on us? It's you that wants it.'

He's right, but I'm too fat now and I like to fool myself that it is for the customers.

I have an electric corn popper, a gift from Jimmie. I get it from the cupboard behind the bar. I spread paper towels on one of the cold boxes, bring out the oil, salt and paper plates. Soon there is the smell of freshly popped corn to greet newcomers.

I hear a few protests.

'I've just had dinner.'

'It gets in my teeth.'

'I'm too bulgy now.'

Most of them succumb. They reach for just one kernel and soon they are eating with the rest of them. I keep the popper going until I get too busy or until everyone seems satisfied.

'Helen, do you want a break?' one of the boys will say now and then.

I am glad for a chance to go around the end of the bar and sit on the customers' side. Any of the regulars who relieve me know where the different brands of beer are kept. They are very, very careful when they make change from the register.

Bobbie, who has done this quite often, has an act of hustling. He tells them to drink fast, and I have to remind him at times that there may be some who think he is in earnest and may resent being hustled. All who know him take it as he means it—an act.

Any time a party is planned, there are advance volunteers as helpers. I do not stay behind the counter on our few party nights. I serve the food from the table in the back of the room while someone tends bar.

I use a lace tablecloth, have candles in holders decorated with bows or flowers. There are stacks of paper plates, plastic forks and napkins.

We try to have one hot entree served in a chafing dish. The rest of the items are sliced meats, cheeses, relishes and spreads.

A couple of times I have had an electric roaster with a real dinner. Once we had cabbage rolls served with sour cream. It was well received, but the room was permeated with the smell of cabbage. Even a deodorant spray could not kill it entirely.

Another time I made a roaster full of spaghetti. We served garlic bread. Gil, who lives a block away, heated it in his oven and rushed portions over at intervals.

In spite of advance notices of buffets, so many eat their dinner before coming. So I decided to limit the buffets to items that did not need to be heated.

Last Thanksgiving Eve we had sliced turkey and sliced ham, both served cold. Relishes, black bread and potatoes scalloped in cheese sauce and served from the chafing dish completed the menu.

It is against the liquor control ruling to advertise and serve free food. It is considered an inducement to drink. However, they are not critical if I don't do it too often.

Four or five times since I have operated the bar, I have masqueraded as an undesirable customer and have been able to deceive the boys for a while. Each time I have planned this I have asked one of the boys to tend bar while I go for dimes or to buy more snacks. I use any excuse to be out of the bar for 15 minutes.

Once I dressed as I thought a female wino would look. I shuffled, bumped into one of my best customers, who was quite indignant, verbally.

I asked another to buy me a beer. He refused me. I heard someone who was sitting in a booth say, 'Oh, my gosh!' I knew by the tone of his voice that he recognized me.

I demanded draft beer from the bartender. We don't carry it and he tried to tell me so.

I was noisy and obnoxious.

Finally I was detected and the patrons were hilarious.

On one of my nights off, some of us went slumming. I saw an old woman, in a dive, selling gum. I thought, 'That's for me.' Shortly after that I copied her appearance.

I wrapped bath towels around me until I had a feather bed figure, donned an old long coat, covered my hair with a dirty turban. I walked into the bar with my eyes cast down, shaking the box of gum under the customers' noses. I didn't speak. My voice would have given me away. No one looked directly at me. The room has subdued lighting and no one knew me.

After having my fun I confessed and three of the boys insisted I go with them to another gay bar which was not too far away. When we pulled up in front, I waited outside until they went in and got settled with a beer at the bar.

When I walked in I started my routine near the door. The owner spotted me and said, 'No, no, lady. You can't do that in here.'

I walked to her and said 'hello' in my natural voice.

She was miffed at my deception. It taught me a lesson. I vowed to keep my masquerades in my own place from then on.

Gene, who is in the costume business, brought me a Roaring Twenties outfit. Beaded knee-length dress, cloche hat, a wraparound velvet jacket, beaded bag and a long strand of beads.

This time I made no attempt to deceive the customers. Chuck tended bar while I wandered around pulling my chewing gum and swinging my beaded bag.

The neighborhood drunk, who comes in just to get thrown out, chose that night for a visit. Forgetting how awful I looked, I approached him bluntly and said, 'You know you can't come in here. Now get out.'

A startled look came on his face as he recognized me. I guess he thought that I had suddenly gone mad.

He left.

I've been a floozy cadging drinks and a begging gypsy. I have always fooled them all for a while. It's fun for me and I hope a diversion for the patrons.

Now and then one of the customers will catch me in the right mood and we'll hurl insults at each other. This may seem to be a strange way to entertain the customers, but it does. Bob said once, as he bought another beer, 'I ought to go home but I'm afraid I'll miss something.'

My closest associates have learned that sweet talk makes me stiffen into a dignified woman, whereas I love pseudo insults. I throw back a few simulated insults of my own.

About nine o'clock, if there are not many in the place, someone will say, 'Give me a salt shaker, Helen.'

I hand him the shaker and he goes to both doors and sprinkles salt across the door jamb. This is supposed to bring in business and the number of times we have had a wave of customers right after the salt has been shaken has made this ritual a 'must.' Of course, we all know that the timing coincides with the usual gathering of the clan, but it's fun to act superstitious.

Joe, who had not been in town for months, was standing at the end of the counter when Dick asked for the salt.

Joe turned to me and showed surprise at this request.

'What is he going to do with that?'

'He's going to sprinkle it across the door to bring in business.' I was very matter of fact in my answer.

He looked at me as if I had lost my mind.

As it happened, a virtual mob of customers showed up in the next ten minutes. Two at the back door, three in the front door, and several singles.

I was busy for a few minutes getting them served and then I went back to him to catch up on our gossip.

'Has Morton Salt Co. heard about this?' he asked.

'You better buy up several boxes as a back log, because as soon as this secret gets out you won't be able to get any.'

I assured him I had plenty on hand.

I hear of things that have happened to the boys during the day. They usually see and tell the humorous side, even if it wasn't funny at the time.

This incident has nothing to do with the fact that the two boys involved are gay, but it is amusing—to the listener, that is—even if it was not very funny to the two boys.

Hank and Bob have an apartment a few blocks from the bar. Each of them is a quiet person, never attracting much attention while in the room. They just stand around talking to friends.

Hank came in early one evening. By this time he could see the ludicrous side of the incident.

'I wish you could have seen Bob and me last night.'

'Why? What happened to you?'

'Bob and I had been out. Not together. He got home first and he sat on the davenport to smoke a cigarette. He had been drinking and he fell asleep and dropped the cigarette.'

'I know what's coming,' I interrupted.

'No you don't, not all. I came in and I had been drinking too. I saw him slumped over and smoke curling up from the seat. I rushed over, shook him, told him he was on fire and ran out into the hall.

'There is one of those folded fire hoses outside our door. I grabbed the nozzle, pulled the hose into the room and handed it to Bob. I told him to hold it while I turned on the water.

'I turned on the water from the hall and Bob could not hold the hose when the water pressure came on. It was like a slapstick movie. That hose swinging around the apartment like a big snake. All the lamps got turned over. It shot into the dressing room and lots of our clothes got wet. The books were soaked and some of the vases were broken.

'Bob yelled at me to turn it off, but I could not hear what he said and I ran to the door to see what it was he wanted and I saw it all.

'I ran back to turn it off but I was not too sober either, so it took a minute or two for me to turn it off.

'You should see that place! The carpet is soaked. We've got all the heat on and the fans going, trying to dry it out. It leaked downstairs a bit. The ceiling below us is spotted.'

'You're insured, aren't you?'

'The building is, I guess. We aren't. It's a mess.'

He was quite philosophical about it. I can understand why. He is not accident prone, but what I call 'trouble prone.' This was just one more thing.

I have led a colorful life.

Late in an evening as we sit talking one of the regulars will say, 'Tell us about the time you were thrown in jail, Helen,' or 'How was your love life when you sang with the band?'

All of us are happy to talk about ourselves and I accommodate with the requested story. It may be colored by repetition.

They don't care. It's all in fun.

Each YEAR, OPENING DAY OF RACING at Santa Anita Park brought a crackdown on bookmaking in Los Angeles County. As the fellow from whom she bought the bar on Melrose had done, Helen accepted and paid off small horseracing bets. And like her predecessor, Helen was arrested for doing so. It seems she was jailed briefly and the judge dismissed the case with a small fine. This gave Helen her own tale of being "thrown in jail" with which to regale her boys.

Helen's attraction to palmistry and theatrical fun tracked back to her youth in Nebraska. She found a lot of appreciative audiences and collaborators in Los Angeles. In the 1930s Helen staged marionette shows for schoolchildren. She donned her gypsy costume to read palms at school bazaars and neighborhood libraries. "She was just such a far-out character, not your ordinary sweet old mom!" Helen's daughter, Caroline, said. "She was always playing with palms and astrology maps. She said she couldn't tell the future but could read character from the palms, and lots of people thought she was really good at it."

Cheiro, the celebrated astrologer, numerologist, and palmist who died in Hollywood in 1936, instructed his fellow palmists: "Speak honestly, truthfully, yet carefully. . . . Above all things, you must be sympathetic: take the deepest possible interest in every person whose hands you read; enter into their lives, their feelings, and their natures. Let your entire ambition be to do good, to be of some benefit to the person who consults you."

Sympathetic palmistry was at the heart of what Helen calls her "gradual convergence" with gay men. While working for tips as a palm-reading entertainer in nightclubs, she found that she hit it off well with some of the male entertainers. After figuring out that it was because they were homosexual that they impressed her as different, she became curious about their hands. Helen reports that her systematic exploration of gay men's hands revealed "a pattern of characteristics visible in almost every hand," but she does not divulge the particulars.

There were many features to be considered in reading the hand: the shape of the whole hand and of the fingers and thumbs, the characteristics of thumb and finger joints, the flexibility of the fingers and their length in relation to one another, the length and shape of the nails, the color and complexion of the palm. And then there was reading the palm, which involved interpreting the major lines, the lesser lines, and the several mounts—the fleshy cushions of the palm.

Helen practiced palmistry as a tool of folk psychology. She also believed that the hands could disclose health problems. Since she was an herbalist, it's likely that she sometimes recommended treatments. "Helen was the original hippie," said her grandson, Russ. Deeply engaged by astrology, Helen had friends who would cast the horoscope. "I think she thought she wasn't responsible for anything—it was all up to the planets," her daughter said with a laugh. "I remember fellows over there all the time, using charts to predict where we were going."

Helen attended spiritualistic churches and gathered with friends for séances. She believed that extraterrestrial beings visited Earth, and like Blanche she believed in reincarnation. Concerning the journey of souls, Caroline recalled Helen declaring, "Until we all straighten up and think properly, none of us are going anywhere!"

In their unconventional spiritual beliefs, Helen and Blanche had ample company in the homophile arena. Mattachine member Don Lucas, partner with Hal Call in Pan-Graphic Press, was drawn to astrology and spiritualism. An astrologer offering advice on "psychological problems" advertised in *ONE*, and letters extolling the occult arts appeared in the magazine through the 1950s.

"I am not one of your subscribers, nor am I a homosexual," wrote Mrs. E. of Los Angeles. "I am an elderly married woman. But I am a friend of a number of homosexuals, and so am fairly acquainted with their unique and special interests." In Mrs. E.'s opinion, the magazine was neglecting "the esoteric and occult aspects of homosexuality . . . a field, vast, vital, and utterly important to every homosexual."

"The homosexuals require a closer linkage to metaphysics," wrote Mr. H. in Cincinnati. "A better knowledge and control of the Astral world will solve many of their problems. The gifts of clairvoyance and healing are not restricted to the heterosexual. I know. I have seen this time and again—with awe." From New York City, Mr. O. wrote, "The answer to the riddle of homosexuality is in parapsychology and occultism. Love must be expressed in all its several levels. We are on one of those levels. There will be a time when all is perfected and harmonized. I do believe though that we are emerging from the darkness now."

As Helen's circle of gay friends grew in the 1930s and 1940s, she would invite them to her home for holidays and other occasions. "That was fine with everyone but my grandmother," Caroline said. "Mother would get so mad at her for being unhappy about that." Helen's mother probably had moments of despair to rival those of any homosexual's mother, wondering how she had managed to produce such a queer one.

Hal Call's mother obviously had such moments. In 1950, when Hal was thirty-three, he received a letter from his mother accompanied by a bookmark imprinted with the scriptural verse "The Wages of Sin Is Death." In the letter she wrote, "Now keep this to yourself, but Dad senses something radically wrong with you and your boyfriends. He wanted to talk with you personally, if, he said, you were to give him a chance without some boy hanging around. He didn't like Jack and said he never saw such a boy. . . . Don't tell Dad . . . a thing, . . . this will go to the grave with me if I was you. Don't tell anyone else and for goodness sake don't write silly letters to boys and men. No matter what you think of them in anyway, don't put it on paper. I didn't tell Dad a thing and he asked me a lot. He says you and he are pals and he'll get it out of you. Well, dear son, if you'll take Mother's advice you *won't* confess a thing to him."

Hal understood his mother's reaction as the product of her small-town Missouri background, religious fundamentalism, and antisexual nature. "He really loved his mother but she could not fully accept him," said fellow Mattachine Don Lucas. The understanding and acceptance that Hal and many others did not get from their own parents they sometimes looked for in other elders. Blanche Baker and her husband, William, served as mother and father figures for many of those who worked with them in therapy. Helen readily assumed the role of gal-pal mother figure in many gay men's lives.

Perhaps with an eye toward winning more mothers to the homophile cause, Hal published "Just between Us Mothers," by Mrs. L. R. Maxwell, in the *Mattachine Review*. "When homosexualism 'strikes home,' the result need not be disownment and chaos," he wrote.

Mrs. Maxwell explained: "My son is a homosexual. He knows it and accepts it: I know it and accept him. Together, we have learned to live with it.

"I address this to other mothers of homosexuals in a plea for understanding, and to help you allay your own fears. You fear only that which you do not understand: a molehill of darkness becomes a mountain of black horror when your shocked senses smother any attempt you may make to understand. You strike out in anger and cruelty when your own fears have grown out of proportion. You wring your hands and weep when your love for yourself is greater than that for your son. If you frankly do not love your son, then throw him to the wolves; he may have guts enough to work out his problem for himself. If you do love your son, then in God's name, help him!

"I grew up in a social strata where the word sex was unmentionable, and the word homosexual completely unknown. I only knew that some boys were 'sissy' and did my share of teasing and laughing at them in a smug sense of superiority. Years afterward I was suddenly shocked to realize that my own son was one of those 'sissies.' . . .

"Why are you so shocked? Well, obviously you have a social misfit on your hands. Nature's laws, and our own social mores, demand marriage and reproduction of our own kind. With the realization that your son will not fulfill these laws comes a sense of social ostracism that is rather overwhelming. What will people say? How can you ever explain that you will never have any grandchildren to show off, to baby-sit, and to spoil? How to bear the fact that he doesn't like girls and prefers the company of boys. Well, face it: these are the facts and you can't wish them away, or hide your head and pretend they are not there.

"What can you do about it? First, you can ask yourself carefully and honestly:

"1. How much of these feelings of fear are based on my own desires rather than on his?

"2. How much am I trying to live his life for him?

"3. Do I feel secure enough in my own family, neighborhood and society to need to care what other people say?

"4. Do I really love my son enough to help him?

"5. Can I just sit back and wait for him to 'outgrow' it?

"If you can answer these questions honestly you have prepared a positive background for some active work. The next step is to try to understand what makes your son the way he is. . . . There are many excellent books and articles on the subject. If you really want to know, you'll find them, read them, and digest them. If you need outside help because you feel inadequate to face it alone, there are professional avenues available. There are doctors to consult; many of the clergy are scientifically trained; there are local civic counseling agencies.

"Your own son can help you to understand, if you can talk freely with him. In fact, he will welcome the opportunity to explain to you how he feels and what he wants. Indeed, it is the thing he most needs: someone to talk with, someone who cares, someone with whom he can be himself. And what better, what more wonderful thing in the world than to talk with his own mother or father! Your son may not know any more than you may know what to do about it. And certainly he is just as frightened and insecure. So, what more glorious thing than to agree to try to work it out together, or to seek outside help together.

"As you begin to work with your son you will find some of the following things are probably true. First (and many psychiatrists agree) you will find that your son has somehow failed to identify with his father. Each of us has some masculine and some feminine traits. Your son has developed his feminine traits at the expense of his masculine because he has not had the opportunity to develop the masculine. The causes of this vary with individuals. You will have the challenge of finding out what is true in your particular experience.

"Second, you may find that you have protected him too much in your own expression of mother love. It so often becomes 'smother love.' . . . You have probably not cut the apron strings sufficiently to allow him his own initiative in daily activities. If this is true I assure you that it is not an easy thing to face. It means facing yourself as much as facing the situation. And it is a difficult thing to accomplish: it may take years of hard work. . . . Does that scare you into doing nothing? Then I can only repeat that you do not really love your son!

"Third, you can help your son to face the thing in himself which has allowed the above conditions to work in him to the end result of homosexuality. For you must not take all the blame: you'll founder in feelings of guilt if you do. Not all overly mothered boys become homos. There is something within the individual that is partly responsible. . . .

"One last word about homosexuals as a minority group. . . . Many of them are highly intelligent and talented. And they can bring those talents to fruition when they are openly accepted, when they do not have to spend their energies in hiding and putting on false fronts of heterosexuality. And I use this last analogy with purpose: they are a gay group in more ways than one. You will find a delightful sense of humor in that son of yours, one that will lighten the hard task of working together. Above all, preserve or cultivate your own sense of humor and ability of having fun. . . . When you reach the point where you have infectious joy together you will know that you are over the hump."

Mrs. Maxwell may have been over the hump, but most American parents were far from being infected with joy on this matter. A more accurate reflection of parental concerns was an ominous 1957 Fort Worth, Texas, newspaper article, "Homosexuality Increasing, Expert Says." The increase was said to be evident not only in teenage girls wearing their hair shorter and boys wearing theirs longer, but also in girls fawning over male celebrities with feminine characteristics while boys were getting crushes on female movie stars with masculine characteristics. "This is what really scares me," said the psychologist who discussed these findings at a Texas law enforcement conference.

In the psychologist's view, it was a "situation caused by World War II and Korea, where children were left with the mother in complete control." He also blamed high divorce rates. "This concept is difficult to accept until you understand that homosexuality is a symptom of hate," he explained, "—the male child for the mother and the female for the father." But he assured his audience that homosexuality could be cured. "So far we've had

100 percent success with 28 cases tested. If we can keep the subject away from the mother (or father in cases of females) for at least a year, we've got the problem licked."

A prominent proponent of curing homosexuals in the 1950s was psychiatrist Edmund Bergler. In her letter to *ONE*, Mrs. S. in Kansas City, Missouri, was spirited in her desire to defend gays against his methods: "Your attack on Dr. Bergler and his book *1000 Homosexuals* was marvellous, and I say bravo, more power to you. . . . I have only read Dr. Bergler's book halfway through, but couldn't wait to finish it before writing you. He must have had some terrible experience himself which has caused him to try to even the score for himself by drilling it into the Gay people that they are masochists and other negative nonsense that is so false. He approaches his patients in such a negative, brutal way. Have you any suggestions as to how I as a Mother and a friend of Gay people could go about helping to expose and get rid of this terribly dangerous man, Dr. Bergler? I have even lost sleep over this."

"I am not of the Gay World, but 'straight,'" wrote another activist mother in Kansas City, Mrs. R. "I have one child, a 22 year old boy, who has been gay since he was 14 years old. I have known about this since last April. Since then I have made his life my life. My husband and I have a large three-story house and are filling our house with Gay boys. So far we have six who are rooming and boarding with us. The people I have known so far of the Gay World are wonderful, talented, fascinating people. I love them all. Since they have come to our home they are much more settled down, much happier and more secure. In our home they know they can be themselves and are protected.

"What a pity there cannot be more 'straight' people who understand and accept Gay people. My son says I know more about Gay Life and homosexuality than a lot of Gay people do. I am trying to write a book, in order to bring better relationships between parents and children of the Gay World. We have had parties in our home accommodating 24 to 30 at a time that were talked about for months afterward. They were nice, decent parties, where they can have drinks and be themselves."

From La Crescenta, California, came a similarly effusive letter from Mrs. K., who signed her name "Bubbles": "I have a grandson who is homosexual and I have come to understand his problems. For many years I have been interested and fascinated by 'the gay world.' I have found that these misunderstood, unaccepted people are wonderful. They have a great deal more kindness than is ever spoken of.

"I have opened my home to them, where they can come and bring their friends. An evening is spent in listening to hi-fi music, singing, dancing, or putting on a little theatrical show. Refreshments are always served. It is wonderful to see and to hear their laughter. They surely 'have a ball.' It is just like one big happy family. Some come to discuss their problems, and everyone offers suggestions.

"If more people would open their homes to them, I believe it would bring a better understanding of these persecuted people. These boys and men have given me the nickname of 'Bubbles' because I am short and fat, which is why I sign it so."

An article by Leah Gailey, mother of a gay son, urged homosexuals to overcome their fears and tell their parents about themselves. "If all parents knew of the homophile problems of their children, it would eventually mean . . . a tremendous spread of understanding and facing of the situation," she stated. She exulted in imagining the "human earthquake" that would occur if at some appointed hour "every homophile, simultaneously, would inform his parents of the facts of his (or her) life." Mrs. Gailey gave tips on how to bring up the topic: "Appraise your parents carefully, prepare the groundwork slowly, and then gently and sincerely tell them." She suggested talking points: "A bit of history of the homophile through the ages, a few statistics culled from Kinsey or other authorities, a smattering of psychology." She also discussed ways to handle rejection: "As calmly as possible, tell them that you intend to live your own life, that you have a right to do so, that you accept the responsibilities for yourself, that you will endeavor to spare them further 'disgrace' by conducting yourself with dignity and consideration . . . within the framework of your own personality." The *Mattachine Review* saluted Mrs. Gailey as "Mother of 1958." That year, she participated with Blanche Baker and Hal Call in a radio panel discussion, "The Homosexual in Our Society."

Here and there across the country, mothers were beginning to speak out and take action in support of their gay sons. And mother-figure allies like Helen and Blanche were beginning to come forward. Of these allies, none made a more significant contribution than psychologist Evelyn Hooker. At the urging of a gay man with whom she had become friends in the 1940s, Hooker began her rigorous, groundbreaking research. Her report of no difference in psychological adjustment between homosexual and heterosexual men jolted the American Psychological Association in 1956.

Back in Los Angeles after the Chicago conference, Evelyn Hooker met with a group of her research subjects at a Hollywood restaurant. "I had promised the gay men that I would let them know what the results were," she said. "Oh, they were uproarious with laughter. 'This is great. We knew it all the time!' I didn't meet with the straight men. They didn't have the motivation to follow an old lady around."

9

'. . . I read her beads for her . . .'

There is one trait, that most of the boys have, that I deplore. It is that they do not want to fight with their families or friends or even in business and the outcome is that they get 'taken' over and over again.

I understand this attitude to some extent. I hate a fight but when I feel that I have had enough, then I am a nasty fighter. My complaint is that they don't feel it worthwhile to finally get mad.

Maybe they achieve results in their own way.

The most noticeable imposition is that made by the family on the unmarried son. He is making good money and the family thinks he might as well have the responsibility of the mother or father.

I hear variations of this theme all the time.

These boys love their mothers, more so than other members of the family, so they invite imposition. They invite it in all their activities. I do not always sympathize when I hear these tales of unfair treatment. I scold, tell them to do something about it, and not complain to me.

Anyone who owns and operates a bar has to have something to sell in addition to the alcoholic beverage. Large cocktail bars sell entertainment and glamour. The small neighborhood bars are meeting places for the gang. The beers are relaxing, the company stimulating. Not many people

111

go to a bar with the purpose of getting drunk. That may be the result when they stay too long. If one really wants to down troubles, the cheapest and quickest way is to buy a bottle, go home and consume it.

Gay bars serve their purpose. They are meeting centers for homosexuals, who want to meet and talk with their own kind.

There are as many different levels in gay bars as there are in straight bars. Some gay bars cater to the screaming exhibitionists. A large percentage of gay fellows would never be seen in such a place.

Most gay boys like to go to a place that is crowded. The talk is stimulating. They can forget their loneliness for a time.

I try to sell safety. Comparative safety, that is.

Principally, I mean safety from entanglement with the vice squad. But also safety from hustlers. These hustlers and spongers count on a gay person taking punishment without daring a complaint, and steal from them without fear of retribution. My demand that any newcomer be sponsored by a regular keeps these parasites at a minimum.

I remember a small fellow who came in three times before I told him not to come back. He was quiet and bought the more costly beer. But he wore suits that were too large for him. Each time he came in he wore a different suit. They were all too broad through the shoulder. The sleeves hung half way on his hand. The pants sagged on his instep. I felt certain that he had gone home with someone and cleaned the closet before leaving. Few weeks pass that I do not hear of these thieveries.

Gordon looked glum as he ordered his beer one evening.

'Take a look at me, Helen. These are all the clothes I own.'

'Who did you take home?' My voice had no pity.

'I didn't take anyone home,' was the answer. 'It's that roommate of mine. He brought a sailor home and the next morning all *my* clothes were gone. He was nearer my size than Jerry's.'

'Is Jerry going to replace your wardrobe?'

'He jolly well is.' Gordon sounded firm.

'Has he that kind of money?' I was skeptical.

'He's going to make a loan.'

'I hope that you insist that he does. Don't get tenderhearted.'

I did not follow up on this story. My guess would be that Gordon got one suit, a couple of shirts and a promise, and that's all.

I do not tolerate anyone who shows by his actions that he is in there just to see what he can pick up.

The bar is a clubby place and I intend to keep it that way.

There are lots of gay bars that welcome anyone and ask no questions except one, 'Can you pay for this beer?' I advise the cruiser to go there.

I do not always spot hustlers and deadbeats immediately. But I do have a good memory. Most of the time I know if the patron has been there before. I have to satisfy myself that I identify him as well as recognize him.

I am pretty cool until I can remember who brought him in, but anyone who has been introduced to me has been warned that this may happen. I tell him to remind me of his previous visit. After a time I introduce him to his neighbor.

This is not always a welcome service. Fred said, after one such introduction, 'I hope you do not mind if I am not social. I just want to sit and watch.'

'I gathered that after I introduced you to Al the other night. You don't have to talk to anyone, of course. I won't do it any more.'

He meant it. He sits, talks to me, consumes a couple of beers and goes.

Not everyone who comes in wants beer. I have many soft drink customers. The first time they order a soft drink, they are apologetic, but I assure them that I have a higher mark up on the soft drinks than on beer.

Because I am a woman, those who want to get by with actions that would not pass in the bar think that the men's room is the place for that. I have news for them. My regulars realize that the men's room is a danger spot. They monitor it for me. If there is any carrying on in there, I am informed immediately. I take the offender to one side, tell him I have complaints and that I don't want to hear any more. This usually solves the problem. The men's room is composed of a large anteroom and a small cabinet that accommodates one person at a time. Unless the bar is real busy, the fellows do not follow one another in. They know I watch, that I have a suspicious mind and they cooperate.

One night a stranger hurried in, leaned over the counter, and whispered, 'Can I use the men's room?'

I was very cold. 'I guess you can. It is not a public toilet, however.'

He went back and he stayed and he stayed and he stayed.

I tried to keep an eye on the door to keep anyone else out. I relaxed my vigilance for a moment. Kent, who had been in close conversation with Harland, had not noticed all this. He went to the men's room. I saw him just as the door swung shut. I was worried. I was about to send Bob in there to prove that three is a crowd, when Kent came out.

I spoke to him over the counter. 'Did that guy make a pass at you?'

'He sure did. Do you want to know what he did?'

'Yes.'

He told me.

I saw red. I stalked toward the back of the room. As I did, the conversation stopped. It was quite obvious there was going to be a scene and no one wanted to miss it.

I flung the door to the room wide open and stood in the doorway. Of course the man in there did not expect to see a woman entering the room and he stood still.

I exploded.

'What do you mean by staying back here and making passes at customers? Come out of there right now and get out of here!'

I followed him all the way to the door yelling at him like a fishwife, but I can't tell what I said. I don't remember. I was too furious to know what I was saying. I think he won't be back, though.

In spite of my happy association with the gay group, I am not blind to their weaknesses. I am not thinking of personal weakness. I am thinking of traits that seem prevalent in the group.

They lie easily and convincingly. This is easy to understand. It is part of their protective pattern. There are hours they cannot account for. They have to make up reasons for being with other fellows and invent reasons for why they don't like this girl or that one.

This unsuspected second life is surrounded by danger. The straight person cannot imagine what it means to live one life for the public, yet have another life that is more real and ardent than the public life.

'Why doesn't he get out of it then?' you may ask.

He can't. He's that way. Some struggle to change. They go to clinics. They marry women. They act as alcoholics, who go on the wagon for six months or a year and then break over into the old habit.

I try not to demand explanations from them nor ask nosy questions. I think I am not lied to, at least not very much.

They cannot extend themselves emotionally. They seem to play at being in love. Possibly they want so much from real love, they are afraid of getting hurt. The excessive idealism, which is their most common trait, spurs them to seek a love that is perfect. And there is no such thing.

I know one who is musical, paints, writes and who has been hunting for years for a companion who is artistic. He has never found his ideal. He strives for perfection in his artistic fields but now he is a complete cynic about love. He cannot accept anything short of perfection in love.

Gay Bar

10

'. . . listen to your mother . . .'

My straight friends often ask me how these boys got started. They want to know if the boy has been seduced by an older man. At what age did he know he was homosexual? Why does he stay in this life?

I do not have any pat answers. There is a pattern of early rearing with many of the same incidents showing, but many heterosexuals have had the same background.

Being in the armed forces introduced many to this life, but that is not the answer either. The larger percentage of service men came back heterosexual. There are many books, written by experts, filled with case histories. Environment seems to be an important factor.

Clinics and psychiatrists are kept busy by folks asking for help. The boys go through the courses outlined for them *but* they are in my place talking it over, with much praise for the course.

I have sympathy for their loneliness. They are missing so much when they renounce normal life. The one big hurdle is their fear of being hurt too much if they get involved in family life. Yet most of them adore children and many talk of marrying only to have children.

When I am curious enough to question, I find some of the following elements in every story.

The most prevalent factor is the mother. In fact I used to think that the mother was the prime factor. Most of the time there is a close sympathy for the mother. Perhaps the father is brutal or neglectful and the boy's love goes to his mother. Other times the mother is a demanding woman and runs both her husband's and her son's lives.

Later I began to see that the boy longs for the love of a man because of a father rejection. Perhaps this rejection is not a conscious one. The father is too busy to bother with the son. He says it is the mother's job to raise children. One of my customers told me the other night of a conversation he had with his father. He was 22 and his father had discovered he was gay. After a long discussion the father said, 'I think it is my fault. I can remember only one time when you and I had an outing together.'

After the boy is old enough to be interested in girls, he carries a fear of getting too involved. His home life has not been happy and he does not want to tie himself to a life of unhappiness similar to his early days.

He thinks he cannot bear having a home life that is not perfect. He knows that if his homosexual home life falls short of his idea of perfection, he can run away without legal proceedings.

He thinks he cannot bear having a heterosexual home life that is not perfect. He wants a lovely home, an attractive wife, peace and quiet and yet this is not always enough.

I have in mind Bob and Ruth. I can say that all the foregoing requirements have been filled for them, but I am afraid he is on his way toward breaking up this marriage.

He and Ruth come in together.

She is beautiful. She knows his former state of being gay. She is financially independent. Most of all she is determined to help him find himself.

He is bored. He hates to spend so much time reading aloud to her or having her read to him. He wishes he could have two or three nights a week of bridge. I know if he had these nights of bridge he would wish for something else. I know his history of early life and can understand why he has no sense of stability, why he shuns responsibility. I have talked to him, severely, pulling no punches and he admits I am right. He promises to reform but he never will and sooner or later Ruth will tire of trying and will give up.

Another couple I know are alcoholic. I think their situation contributes to this. He told her he was gay before he married her. Told her he wanted to give it up. She accepted this and wanted to help him. They have children.

She is not neat. The house is untidy. These are very important things to him and he helps with the house when he comes home from work. He frets because of these restrictions and drinks. She wants to be a pal and drinks too.

What can you do for them?

Nothing.

Of course you can say they are no more unhappy than any other bored couple, and you are right.

I have no answers to gay problems. I enjoy gay companionship. These fellows are witty, generous and kind. I am at ease with them. I can see they refuse to fetter their emotions. I think it is through fear of pain. Certainly the chief characteristic in this group is sensitivity and idealism. They give me love, but they know I am not going to make demands of this love.

I try to take them as they are and I enjoy the association. I have asked many fellows how they got started in this life.

The popular idea that an older man has seduced a young boy is not often true. I spent one Sunday afternoon on the phone, calling my friends and asking them how they got started.

I had one story of an early first experience with an older man. It was his music teacher and it was so repugnant to him that he avoided all thought and talk of sex for a long time. Later he became interested in girls and all through high school he went for them in a big way. Later still, while in the armed forces, he turned to gay life. His stated reason for this switch was that girls felt that sex was something to hold out as a bait for marriage and that they made no effort to be interesting and entertaining. They bored him.

His attitude is a very prevalent one in the bar. Girls should realize that if sex is their lure for marriage, there is not much to hold the marriage together after the bait is taken. If the inducement is mental stimulation, there is a chance of continued interest.

I think it is a difficult—often impossible—task to change these fellows after they are set in this life. There is an attractiveness in gay life that is similar to the hold of alcohol or dope.

If a fellow marries with all the good intentions in the world, he still cannot forget the carefree life he has left.

When the boy in his teens shows signs of being homosexual, an informed person might be able to help him face himself and his responsibilities. The flaw in this is that not every one can detect this trend, nor can they, with authority, point to the unhappy side of this life.

So many times the finger of shame is pointed toward the group which makes the victim of his own nature become defiant and say, 'It's the way I am and I can't help it.'

I think that some or all of the following traits are present in every patron of my bar: Extreme idealism; sensitivity; an alert and witty mind and, most of all, a determination not to be caught in the maelstrom of an unhappy married life.

My viewpoint is that many people are not the type to be married—whether homosexual or heterosexual. Take them as they are and enjoy their company.

I want to say to mothers and fathers that if you discover that your son is a homosexual, accept it.

I think of George, a friend of long standing, who told me his story. He tired of living the double life, and wrote a long letter, telling his mother the story. He told her he was running away with Jimmie and would not ever see the family again.

He left the letter on the dresser and took his belongings to Jimmie's house. He and Jimmie packed the car and were almost ready to take off.

George's mother came home early from work and found the letter. She took a taxi to Jimmie's place and found them coming out with the last of the boxes. She convinced George that his deviation did not mean a thing to her and persuaded him to come home with her.

George went to a psychiatrist to talk this thing out, and the doctor asked him to send his mother in for a talk. When she went, he talked bluntly to her. He told her it was not possible to change George but that she and her husband should adjust their thinking.

The result is a very happy home life for all of them. I know her well and she is a happy woman.

I mentioned earlier the fellow who has become manager of an ice skating show. His mother once talked to me about this problem. She was serious. She told of her nice relationship with her son and felt sorry for parents who, because of public opinion, had driven their sons from them. We agreed that the parents and not the boys lost from the separation.

If parents have a free conscience, if they feel they have given the boy all their love and understanding, then they should not suddenly point a finger of scorn at him when they discover his deviation.

He cannot help himself. He is more dismayed than they. He has fought himself for years and faces, knowingly, more and more years of loneliness.

If only parents could say, 'We know. We are sorry you are as you are, but you are still our son and we love you,' then there would be one less lonely boy to wind up in a gay bar.

Based on twenty years of getting to know many homosexual men, Helen's assessment of her boys' common traits is insightful. Sometimes quirky and artless, her commentary seems mostly unfettered by considerations of political correctness. Though not always flattering, it is informed by the intelligence and affection of a woman who wrote about her boys candidly and for their own good. She makes it clear that homosexuals aren't the monsters that many imagine, but they do have their shortcomings just like anyone else.

For a woman as ready to get her feathers ruffled in self-defense, it's no surprise that Helen would have deplored her boys' disinclination to stand up for themselves and fight for their own interests. Yet she observes that "the boy who is basically homosexual" tends to be unusually sensitive, neat, and polite. And she notes that a bar that had been a hangout for fist-fighting rowdies became a peaceful place when she began operating it as a gay bar. So Helen probably understood her boys' shying away from confrontation in a larger context: men who were unusually gentle by nature were not likely to be models of assertiveness, especially in a culture that was hostile to their very existence. But their passivity still exasperated her.

It is telling that one of the few productions of the Mattachini Players was a puppet play based on *The Reluctant Dragon*, the Kenneth Grahame fairy tale about a bohemian dragon who writes poetry, tells stories, sings, and hates fighting.

"*They never fight back!*" said Donald Webster Cory. "That, more than anything else, is characteristic of the discrimination against homosexuals. They accept, quietly and willingly, only too happy that they have been spared the humiliation of exposure. They accept, with head bowed—angry, hurt, and helpless—and often with some sense that perhaps their lot is not entirely without justification."

"Until the colored people fought for their rights they got nowhere," stated Mr. A. of Upper Darby, Pennsylvania. "The only reason that I can see for homosexuality being scorned by the people is that the homosexual will not get up and fight for his ideas and beliefs." A *Village Voice* writer stated, "Homosexuals *as a group* aren't going to lead any revolt because the last thing they want is to get involved in any real struggle. They just want to be let alone to lead their precious lives in their presently established dainty fashion."

A letter to the *Mattachine Review* conveyed the mindset of self-deprecating acquiescence. "Yes, I am as much of a variant as the next one," said Mr. A.V. in California, "however the term 'gay' is about as misleading as calling an ugly duckling a swan. . . . Surely we must quit whimpering about our lot when we know full well that ALL other human beings have many adjustments to make. Rather shouldn't we so live and be as tolerant in our attitude toward those whom we feel are oppressing us, as to be more readily acceptable to them?"

Addressing the gay penchant for lying that Helen remarks on, a *Mattachine Review* article proposed an assertive response to conformist pressure. "Lying and hypocrisy are the results of fear, no matter how well they may be disguised," the author stated. "We need not bear banners on our sleeves proclaiming what we are, but neither do we have to hang our heads in shame or try to be something we are not. It's about time we began to act as though we were sure of ourselves.

"Lately when some nosey neighbor asks me why I haven't married, I tell him politely but firmly that it's none of his business. Why should I make up some ridiculous story about a girl I'm going with? I have lots of girl-friends but I think too highly of them to use them as alibis, to parade them around on my arm as if to say to the world 'See, I'm not gay, after all. I have a girl!' And when people actually have the gall to come right out and ask me whether or not I am homosexual, I have recently found it impossible to refrain from telling the truth, even in the most embarrassing circumstances. At least I have the satisfaction of watching them squirm when it was they who expected me to lie and squirm. I feel that anyone who goes this far in his interrogation has already made up his mind anyway, and no matter what you say, he will not change his mind. Why add further ignominy to yourself by lying?

"In short, let's put an end to the bad reputation we have given ourselves. No matter how much we may be despised, let us at least show the world that we have some idea of honor among ourselves, and that as individuals we have not lost our integrity and self-esteem."

In Helen's eyes, her boys' most common trait is idealism that is "extreme," even "excessive." She considers this the cause of much of their unhappiness in love. In their quest for "a love that is perfect," they do not "extend themselves emotionally"; they "seem to play at being in love." Striving for perfection, these men often achieve impressive results in their professional and creative endeavors but seldom in their romantic lives. Extreme idealism would also seem to be at the root of their perfectionism in the homemaking arena. Pity the woman who finds herself married to a fastidious homosexual!

Among her boys, an "alert and witty mind" was a common trait of which Helen approved completely. In fact, a large part of her attraction to running the bar was all the fun she had—the quick repartee and campy one-liners, the colorful stories and jokes, the masquerading, the pseudo-insulting banter and overall giddy vibe.

Gay men's predilection for wittiness is evident in letters to *ONE*. In the same 1953 issue in which a reader suggested leaving the word *homosexual* off the magazine's cover because "it strikes terror into the hearts of so many homosexuals," another reader suggested publishing some lighter material: "Let's face it, fellows: life is tough, but not THAT tough. At least, not all the time." This was at the height of the nation's McCarthyist convulsions, with homosexuals being purged from government employment as subversives, possibly Communists. Who couldn't use a good laugh?

"Lately I've read ONE and felt quite thoughtful and serious," wrote Mr. A. in Los Angeles, "then read your sister publication Mattachine Review and felt downright down-in-the-mouth with NO feeling of even hope. There's nothing so healthy as a good laugh and a laugh at one's self is even more beneficial. Life demands crusaders and tears, but the sane 'normal' life also demands comedians and laughter."

Like many *ONE* readers, Mr. S. in Fort Worth longed for the magazine to be spiced with even more fun and whimsy and cleverness. "That your motives and editorial policies are serious and dedicated is highly commendable," he wrote, "but in the process of taking yourselves so seriously, *One* frequently reads like a newsletter from a leper colony. . . . Most gay people are blessed with a well-developed and rare sense of humor, more so, in fact, than many so-called normal people. A little lighter editorial approach would give your magazine a whale of a goose, and probably be a lot more effective. After all, it's easier to read and remember one of Oscar Wilde's or Noel Coward's barbed witticisms than some legislator's political tirades."

A psychotherapist whose workdays must have been enlivened by many a barbed witticism reported that American homosexual culture was characterized by three key beliefs: "(1) that homosexuality is incurable (2) that homosexuals are inherently superior to heterosexuals, and (3) that the homosexual life is more exciting, more romantic, more exhilarating, more wonderful, more 'out-of-this-world' than anything that can be offered by the dull, drab, dreary, deadly world of heterosexuality." He summarized the way gay men verbalized these beliefs as: "(1) you can't do anything about yourself anyhow, but why should you want to?—you are (2) better than other people and (3) have a much better world opened up to you than if you were on that 'vulgar heterosexual kick.'"

Helen states that many of her boys sought help from clinics and psychiatrists in their efforts to make a heterosexual adjustment. "The boys go through the courses outlined for them *but* they are in my place talking it over, with much praise for the course," she says ironically. This is a fascinating glimpse of American gays in a time of momentous transition. Beginning to imagine their own authority and integrity, they could not truly believe in it or assert it until they had gone further in rejecting the anti-homosexual dictates of several major forces of conformity, the psychotherapists in particular. So Helen's boys would go dutifully to their appointments, then gather in her gay bar to chat favorably about their adventures in psychotherapy.

In remarking on her boys' extraordinary love for their mothers, Helen surely realized that her own bonds with them grew out of their affinity with mother-figures and other female elders. Helen's comments on "how these boys got started" as homosexuals show that she was well aware of the prominent role of the mother in prevailing psychoanalytic theories. In Cory's list of nine "causes of homosexualism," mother figured prominently in the top four: "1. Unbalanced love of a boy for his mother, reaching heights of physical desire from which there is a subsequent flight. 2. Effort of a boy to replace his father because of the latter's absence, death, or inadequacy, with all heterosexual love representing the love for his mother. 3. Identification of a boy with his mother, resulting in an effort to be like her in every respect. 4. Lack of love from the mother, or loss of mother, with the boy seeking to play the role of wife and lover in the psychic relationship with the father."

Kinsey's revelation that the scope of homosexuality in America went far beyond the occasional obvious swish heightened an existing preoccupation with causes and cures. The resulting burst of theorizing and experimentation had damaging consequences for many gays. But even by the early 1950s psychotherapists were beginning to discard the idea that homosexuals could be changed to heterosexuals. "The psychiatrists . . . will tell the invert, or his mother, that he can be helped," said Cory. "But, on investigation, I find that their help consists of his making a better adjustment as a homosexual, and not of overcoming the drive. Sometimes the therapist will bring about a heterosexual adjustment, leading in fact to a happy marriage, but this does not involve a diminution of the homosexual drive."

Helen states that "why" is the biggest word in her vocabulary, but her statements on the why of homosexuality are quite insubstantial. In part this was due to the era's sprawling hodgepodge of conjectured causes. No one could have made sense of it. Further, it seems that why wasn't really so important to Helen in this matter. She connected with gay men as friends—witty, generous, kind companions with whom she felt at ease. "I have no answers to gay problems," she states. For Helen, a decided nonconformist who knew the sting of disapproval and rejection, what mattered most was doing what she could to make life better for her boys while having some fun.

Similarly, Blanche wanted to help each individual understand and accept himself and become as well-adjusted as possible. Most of the gay men who sought Blanche's help wanted to go straight. "I always tell them that if they have a heterosexual component large enough to function with . . . they may be able to marry or have a love affair with a person of the opposite sex," she explained. "But in so many cases they don't have that potential, and I just simply have to work with what we have."

Consistent with Blanche's ideas about helping homosexuals in their adjustment were the thoughts of Mr. R.E.D., a Californian who said that his pet peeve was the idea of curing homosexuals: "How foolish! Can you cure brown eyes? Or love of music? Or slenderness of a healthy body? There's no illness in homosexuality itself. Articles defending deviates should never refer to curing them but might well discuss making better conformists out of them—or steps leading to better judgment and discretion and more understanding of the value to all of us—deviate or 'normal'—of good behavior in public places. But please, no cures!"

Making better conformists out of homosexuals was at the heart of the 1950s marriage imperative. There was nothing new in this—since the invention of marriage, lots of homosexual men had been marrying women. But the marriage push took on heightened intensity as American popular culture enshrined the nuclear family. "Our society is preoccupied with family life, and anyone who is not so preoccupied is seen as a lesser person," wrote Donald Webster Cory and John LeRoy. "Single men and women are looked upon with disfavor, while the family man and the loyal wife are seen as pure, wholesome, and virtuous."

"God! Mother was unrelenting," Hal Call said of that period, when he was in his thirties and not even pretending an interest in marriage. "'You're missing the dearest thing in your life by not having a dear wife and little ones to care for.' We were very close, but her life was centered on God, Jesus, the church, and family: 'With a family you really have something to work for; you'll love to do it . . . and with these grandbabies—well, I just have twice as much to live for.'"

"Is marriage the answer to the problem of the struggle for adjustment of the homosexual in a hostile world?" asked Cory. "This is a question which almost every gay person has asked himself on numerous occasions and which he can answer only for himself." To Mr. C.M. in Massachusetts, the answer was looking like yes. In a letter to Blanche he explained that he had always tried to live discreetly but hostile attitudes toward homosexuals were causing him to consider getting married as a cover-up: "Recently I met and have been courting a country girl who is beautiful but dumb and I hope to get married soon. Already I have noticed people's attitudes changing toward me. People who formerly wouldn't speak to me now go out of their way to be friendly. But I ask you, have I proven to be a coward by taking this step or just wise? Is it wrong for me to channel my passions and desires along the accepted lines? I am gay and I always will be, but with effort I can manage to perform as an acceptable husband."

Blanche had no illusions of this fellow's chances for success: "I am sure that many readers of this column have tried the same 'escape' method and can tell you what an unsatisfactory solution this was."

Considering the culture of the times, one might assume that a leading reason for gay men to get married would have been bridling, if not banishing, their homosexuality and fitting into the social order. Cory did not think that was the case. "It would seem from my observation that first and foremost is the homosexual dominated by a desire to have children," he said. "This wish is likely to be stronger in the invert than in others, and certainly it plays a greater role in a decision to get married." Similarly, Helen remarks of her boys that "most of them adore children and many talk of marrying only to have children." Another observer stated that "many homosexuals tend to sentimentalize the heterosexual way of life, the 'wife, home and babies' routine. There is always a tendency, it seems, to compare the ideal married life with the homosexual life at its worst."

In stating that "there is an attractiveness in gay life that is similar to the hold of alcohol or dope," Helen acknowledges the unalterable nature of sexual orientation. "'All you need is a woman!' You know, as well as I, that a woman will never solve the problem of your desire for men," Cory said. "On the other hand, you yourself, for a variety of reasons . . . , may decide to embark upon a course of marriage. If it is possible to do so with a mate who understands your nature and who will not consider it a threat to her position, the possibilities of a successful marriage are not at all remote."

Though many gay men married in the hope of eradicating their homosexuality, the idea of "adjustment through marriage" had various interpretations. "It is true that many homosexuals would like to be able to marry and cohabit with women, beget children, and live 'socially normal' lives,"

Cory stated, "but this does not mean that they want to relinquish their libidinous drive." It seemed to him that outside of the gay world few people realized "how many of these homosexually-inclined bisexuals marry, and how much homosexuality is practiced or desired among married men." For some homophiles, the fact that many homosexuals were married enhanced the image they wished to project of the homosexual as a normal man.

Another observer noted that some decidedly homosexual men "may marry, have children, and even become satisfactory husbands or lovers for those complaisant women who can understand and accept their extramarital homosexual venturing. It is mostly within this category that homosexuals may be found whose attentions are preferred by no small number of sophisticated women because they 'understand women' and because, incidentally, and for reasons that are not obscure, sexual activity before orgasm may be so indefinitely prolonged that the female companion can attain maximum physical satisfaction."

Still, many gay men never married and some boldly rejected the idea that the absence of "sex-love involvements with members of the other sex" was a sign of mental illness. Mr. P. in Los Angeles reflected this self-assured mindset: "I say Dr. Albert Ellis is a jerk. Why should any Gay person have to have sexual relations with the opposite sex if it is against his nature? I have only one question I would like to ask this Ellis character, and that is, 'How many shades of gray are there betwixt white and black?'"

More scathing were Val Richardson's comments after his years as a lay religious counselor in Southern California: "If you think homosexuals have adjustment problems, you ought to spend a few years listening to the woes of the young-marrieds, with their in-laws, their budget worries, their endless infidelities or near-infidelities. Or, even worse, the middle aged and older heterosexuals, with their pitiable fixations on their children and grandchildren, their nasty little sex frustrations, their pallid, hypochondriac emotional patterns. You would be glad to get back into the clean, healthy air of our own way of life."

For the Record

One evening some months ago, just after I had opened for the night, the phone rang.

When I answered, a male voice said, 'Is this Mrs. Branson?'

'Yes,' I replied.

'This is Dr. Kinsey of Indiana University,' he said.

I was excited, but managed to express my pleasure in hearing from him.

He said, 'Mr. Owen wrote me about you, saying you would like to meet me and would be glad to answer my questions.'

The result of this phone call was a one o'clock appointment the next day, at his hotel.

When he came to the door of his sitting room the next day I was surprised. I don't know what type of person I expected to meet. Probably a long-faced person fitting the popular conception of a college professor.

His ready smile and charming manner immediately made me feel at ease. When we were seated, he reached for a writing pad, asking if I objected to his taking notes. I assured him that I did not. We spent one and a half hours in conversation.

Most of that time was spent in answering his penetrating questions.

He had just come from San Francisco and gave me the details of a mass arrest in a small community near there. He told of the flimsy case the authorities had against the accused boys and said it would be interesting to watch for the results. Many of the boys had asked for a jury trial, which was an unexpected move, and, from his view point, showed a growing trend toward courageously admitting homosexuality.

Then we started a question-and-answer conversation.

'Mrs. Branson, why do you prefer owning a homosexual bar?'

The question took some thought for a truthful answer.

'Probably two or three reasons all in one. First, my customers are clean, neat, polite, thoughtful and are easy to handle. I have very few problems with them.

'I worked in regular cocktail bars for years, as an entertainer, and I dislike trying to get along with drunken women. Now, I do not allow un-attended women in the bar, although I welcome any woman brought in by my regular customers.

'Also, the most important reason, I think, is that I can be myself with these boys without misunderstanding. I can be vivacious and yet know that that is not a signal for someone to make a pass at me. Again, referring to my entertainment days, I was so tired of telling someone to keep their hands off me, or assuring some drunk that I did not make a practice of going home with the male customers, that my association with gay fellows is a welcome relief.'

He smiled as he made notes.

'Mrs. Branson, I have received almost identical answers every time I have asked a woman owner of a gay bar for her reason for operating one. Now tell me how you pay off the police.'

'I don't. They don't come in.'

'You surely give someone a free drink or a case of beer, don't you?'

'No, I don't. They don't come in.'

He made his notes and continued.

'Do you hire a bouncer?'

'No, I don't.'

'Don't you need one now and then?'

'No, I go on the theory that offense is the best defense. I am rude to an unwanted character, and because I look like a lady, he is so surprised he just leaves. Anyway if anyone hit me, I think all the fellows in the bar would take him apart.'

He wrote a few lines and had another question ready.

'How do you control the men's room?'

'I don't have to. The boys police it. If anyone gets out of line I hear about it soon. I take the offender aside and warn him that another complaint will result in an eighty-six. This takes care of it.'

We had a discussion about general conditions, comparing this city with different Eastern cities.

His questions and comments were so impersonal and so tolerant that I could not be anything but candid and truthful.

Although I spent only a short time with him, I left feeling that I was leaving an old friend.

There is an amusing sequel to this interview.

A few days later, some members of the Mattachine Society, an organization working with the homosexual problem, were in the bar. They had had a round table conference with Dr. Kinsey on the evening of my interview.

He had told them of our talk and expressed a mild skepticism of my answers. The group assured him that my answers were true.

'Well,' he told these fellows, 'If that woman runs that bar the way she says she does and the way you say she does, then it is the only bar in the United States that is run that way.'

I consider that statement a great compliment.

When I heard of Dr. Kinsey's passing I felt a personal loss and realized also that the homosexual group lost a great and powerful friend.

ALFRED KINSEY'S RESEARCH in human sexuality was shaped by the mindset of the entomologist he had once been. This was a great strength of his groundbreaking work and a great obstacle to the acceptance of his findings. Kinsey and his colleagues presented blunt facts on sensitive topics to a public whose ignorance and insecurity on sexual matters were profound. His report on male sexuality fascinated and infuriated many Americans. Publication of Kinsey's report on female sexuality provoked conservative politicians to attack him as a threat to the nation's integrity and security. Alfred Kinsey struggled to survive the 1950s. By the time he was interviewing Helen and meeting with Mattachine groups in California, he had managed to secure funding for his research on sex offenders.

Helen finished writing *Gay Bar* by June 1956, adding her postscript following Kinsey's death in August. Hal Call tried to secure funds to help with *Gay Bar* production costs. His letter to a prospective lender, a Mattachine member in Ohio, included an assurance: "We would not consider the publication of a book under the highly controversial title it has UNLESS it would serve to amend the erroneous public thinking about places called 'gay bars.'"

Hal and Helen eventually agreed on a shoestring edition of 2,500 copies, of which 1,600 were produced. Upon receiving a request from the story department at Warner Bros. for copies of her forthcoming book, Helen told Hal that she was "beginning to get a little excited about this now," despite her ill-fated venture with the ghostwriter. Her excitement must have been heightened by Hal's news that some fellows in New York would be contacting her about dramatic rights.

Hal and Helen collaborated in designing the book's dust-jacket illustration. The drawing depicts Helen as a stout, matronly hen garbed in spectacles, earrings, and showy hat. She shelters a clutch of agitated chicks under her wings while looking sternly at a police-officer chick who brandishes his nightstick toward a lone wayward hatchling engrossed in tugging on an earthworm. It was "mother hen guarding her little gay chicks," Hal remarked years later. "And here is one that is out there too busy pulling on the worm—like sex in a public park—and here's the cop! He was too busy getting into sucking dick and didn't see the policeman. She was looking at the cop and giving the cop hell . . . ! She was a king without a penis."

Helen believed that a review of the book in the *Mattachine Review* would be ample publicity. "I think, knowing the grapevine, that it will sell itself," she told Hal. "I plan getting several hundred copies for sale in the bar. I might as well get the dealer's commission as well as my royalty. Money, money, money." Helen traveled to San Francisco in summer 1957 to help promote the forthcoming book at the Mattachine convention. She received her first copies of the slim, three-dollar hardcover in December 1957, three months behind schedule and a month after her mother's death. That the edition included some numbered copies with a special autograph page indicates the book's special significance for both Helen and her publisher. "To my favorite *author* and my favorite *Gay Bar*," Hal inscribed Helen's copy. "Your first is our first also. Here's hoping we can both create a second as successful as this one looks right now!"

Pan-Graphic advertised the book in the *Mattachine Review* and sold copies by mail. *Gay Bar* was also sold by the ONE Book Service in Los Angeles; the Winston Book Service in Hempstead, New York; the Village Theater Center in New York City; and several other retail outlets. With help from substantial advance sales, the gay grapevine, and an autograph party in Los Angeles, the books moved quickly. A month after publication Pan-Graphic had fewer than 300 copies remaining, and within a year those sold out. Pan-Graphic did not reprint the book and apparently never paid Helen the agreed-upon royalties. It seems that her proceeds were limited to the roughly $200 she realized from selling copies herself.

Reviews of *Gay Bar* in the homophile press were enthusiastic. "The story moves smoothly and swiftly," said the reviewer for *ONE*, "changing in mood from the hilarious to touching incidents of pathos and maladjustment, but never does the author treat her characters condescendingly or as if they were occupants of some zoo." The introduction by Blanche Baker was deemed "stimulating, provocative." *Gay Bar* was "both entertaining and significant," stated the critic for the *Mattachine Review*. In addition, "By being observant and open-minded, Mrs. Branson has learned a great deal about homosexuality." The critic stated that Helen "writes modestly and simply, with an occasional evocative line," and "all the information and intriguing ideas are conveyed painlessly in one good story after another." In his view, Blanche Baker's introduction "adds considerably to the value of the volume."

Particularly appreciative was a review in *The Ladder*, a lesbian publication: "Though it deals exclusively with the male homosexual and has no direct bearing on Lesbianism per se, it nevertheless tells a much-needed story." The reviewer further stated that *Gay Bar* tells "with fascinating humor and deep compassion (not to mention a good deal of love) the plain truths of the upper echelon of male homosexual society. That side of which is so often neglected or overlooked entirely. This is no spiced-up tale of a limp-wristed set of maladjusted and pitiable boys, but a clean honest story of the decent honorable responsible adult homosexual. This book is not fiction but fact, and undoctored fact as well. Probably the most amazing part of the book is the fact that Miss Branson is apparently one of the so-called 'normal' and therefore her book is objective and not subjective. One more cheer for our side by a sincerely interested outsider." Calling the book a must for collectors of gay literature, the reviewer assured "those of you who do not read the literature generally because of the tone of helpless futility expressed by some of it" that *Gay Bar* "is happy and light-hearted and still retains a logical sense of balance."

In a letter to *ONE*, Mr. P. in Australia reported that *Gay Bar* was "providing a great discussion provoker with my friends, both homosexual and 'square.' A down-to-earth discussion from the inside is so rare, that a book of this sort certainly proves a winner. I shall be writing Mrs. Branson myself to tell her just what sort of an impression her book has made on this side of the Pacific."

However, another Mr. P. was not impressed. "I cannot recall reading a duller, more stupid or unnecessary book," he wrote from Indianapolis. "The author does not even comprehend the actual subject matter of her pamphlet, for a far more suitable title for her very small effort would be 'Ain't I Cute?' I am certain that *ONE*'s promotion of such a low grade manual of self appreciation has done your book department irreparable harm. So far as I can discern, the book begins and ends with Dr. Baker's intelligent and enlightened introduction."

But *Gay Bar* was one of the finest books Mr. E.W.G. in California had ever read: "It was not like a story to me. It was rather like she was sitting across from me in my living room telling me the incidents herself. With this book out . . . , I think she should keep her recorder and start another book. True stories about those around her makes most interesting reading. I hope to see Mrs. Branson someday soon, and I sincerely hope she does not give me the warm glass treatment."

With his interest in true stories of gay lives, this gentleman may have become a fan of Blanche Baker's "Toward Understanding" column when it began appearing in *ONE* a year later. But Blanche died in December 1960, at age fifty-four, so her column lasted only a year and a half. Its final appearance included the only hostile letter she ever published, from "Mrs. Ashamed to Sign" in Fairfield, California. This letter gives a noteworthy glimpse of the powerful antipathy that was emerging as gay men and lesbians were becoming more visible and vocal.

"I'm a true female and proud of it," the letter began. "I can imagine I should have only compassion for you. I would, if I thought you kept your homosexual practices private—surely you don't; you're bold enough to almost shout about them! Perhaps your name in the papers will draw in more companions for you—on your experience couch? Well, more power to you. Only I hope the likes of you never gets her claws into my son—or brothers.

"I can see you now—a voice like a man, a moustache, and perhaps a cigar? (Or are you the pale, sick, confused-appearing, emaciated receiver in this game of 'Disgrace Against God's Plan'?) Let me tell you, Doctor (terrible they've seen fit to give you the title) those of us who have to contend with these homos are not in favor of its promotion, as *you* advertise. True, they need help—but who are you to proclaim that it's alright when an imbecile knows they are sick, sick. It wasn't God's plan of life. Law repulses your teaching. Incidentally, your stinking, lousy low-moralled California is full of them—those rats that molest our children in school here daily, etc. I'll bet $100.00 you have no children. You are low enough to be an animal, with your idiotic views, and not fit to be a parent. I hope you don't have any children."

Blanche's response was pointed but reserved: "I am happy to find that you could find the words to express yourself as frankly as you did about this controversial subject. It must have relieved a lot of guilty and hostile feelings to blow off steam as you did. I wish we might get together sometime to discuss your views; surely there must be reasons for you to feel as you do. I am not trying to say that my views are the only views, but I do feel that it is more worthwhile and productive of better understanding to take a more positive viewpoint and to try to help homosexuals to find outlets for their exceedingly human and natural tendencies.

"Whenever anyone attacks me as you have, I always try to look into the matter carefully to see if there is really anything constructive in what they have to say. In the case of your letter, I'm afraid you missed the boat on most of your points. I am not and never have been a practicing homosexual, although I have deep sympathy for the cause, and am quite bisexual in my clinical interests.

"With best wishes for increased depth of understanding as the years go on."

California was indeed full of homos, and Hollywood was their long-established haven. But Helen was not a witness to its blossoming as a gay capital during the 1960s. By about 1960 she had served her last beer at 5124 Melrose. Helen may have sold the bar to a new proprietor, or it may have gone out of business. Redevelopment soon demolished the building.

Helen moved on, first to Santa Cruz for several years, then to Amador City, a small town in California's historic Gold Country near Sacramento. In a century-old house on Amador Creek with the Siamese cats she adored, Helen lived the frugal, eccentric life of an elderly hippie, listening to classical music, hanging herbs on the porch to cure. Working at a local museum and reading tourists' palms at a small hotel supplemented her Social Security check. "It was clean poverty," said her grandson, Russ. "Granny was poor, but she didn't want, and she had friends. Everybody who lived up in the Gold Country was a little haywire anyway, so it was a good melding of the minds."

When Helen was in her late seventies, her daughter and son-in-law, Caroline and Albert, helped her move to Sacramento. After a brief hospitalization, Helen died there in January 1977. Consistent with her wishes, her family scattered her ashes in Amador City. "She was an extremely different person, and a very difficult person for me, as my mother," Caroline said. "She was a very big embarrassment when I was a teenage girl. But she had lots of fun and friends and enjoyed immensely, and never worried about what the average public was thinking. There were so many things that I felt she should have been doing differently! But I am ever, ever grateful that she taught me to be a freethinker, and not to judge people."

"Helen was a nonconformist long before it was chic to be one," said Russ. "In fact, it was definitely a drawback in her entire life. She dressed differently; she conducted herself differently. She probably felt that she was not of this world, that she was out of place, out of time. Maybe that was part of her affinity for the gay community. Long before anybody thought of it as oppression, she believed that those guys were oppressed."

"She just thought that *something should be done!*" Caroline said of Helen's endeavors on behalf of her gay friends. "She was going to give them a place to congregate and enjoy and be friendly. And she was going to let people know that this had to be accepted. She was a crusader: she was going to reform things."

The homosexual problem" was much debated in America in the 1950s, and the phrase was bandied about earnestly by many homophiles as readily as it was by legal and medical authorities. Many gays blamed themselves for the problem. "It is an undeniable and uncomfortable fact that we homosexuals ourselves are largely responsible for the aura of ignorance and prejudice which enshrouds us," an article in the *Mattachine Review* stated. "We are responsible because of our silence."

But some gays rejected the concept of the homosexual problem. "A sociologist writing on racial minorities . . . has stated that there are no minority problems," said Donald Webster Cory. "There are only majority problems. There is no Negro problem except that created by whites; no Jewish problem except that created by Gentiles. To which I add: and no homosexual problem except that created by the heterosexual society. . . . It is a majority problem, but only the minority is interested in solving it."

"'Homosexual problem,' etc., ad nauseam," Mr. B. in Allentown, Pennsylvania, wrote to *ONE*. "There is not and never has been a homosexual problem. The 'problem' is a vicious state-of-being created by sheep-brains. No one sets out to love the same sex; he/she was created that way. And that the tinkerers are old enough to know, but they glory in ignoring Nature. The 'crime against Nature' is not homosexuality; it is this— THE INJECTING OF ONE'S SNOUT INTO OTHER PEOPLE'S AFFAIRS."

The homophile literature of the 1950s offers several observations as to why American heterosexual culture was seemingly intent on deploying "every device human ingenuity and prejudice can design for frustrating the homosexual, turning him neurotic or, if possible, eliminating him entirely." In Cory's view, "Their need for hatred rises out of a deep sense of insecurity; . . . their disgust comes from a fear that there is the germ of the gay impulse in them."

Before an audience of hundreds at a public meeting in Boise, Idaho, at the beginning of the city's sex-crime panic of 1955–56, psychiatrist John Butler named this fear. "You must take the realistic view that homosexuality is here," he told the audience, "and a little bit of it is probably in all of us." Psychiatrist Karl Bowman went further in a speech before the Commonwealth Club in San Francisco, stating that the homosexual problem might never be solved due to the fear and latent homosexuality in the rest of the population.

"Depth study is needed to determine why there is so much institutionalized and individual hostility toward the homosexual," Cory stated. "What are the hidden conflicts, repressions, and unresolved drives within the normal person that produce so much fear, revulsion, and hostility toward homosexuality?"

In the late 1950s, observers began to note an exaggeratedly butch affect among urban gays. "For every homosexual who feels compelled to 'announce' his existence by slithering down 8th Street, there are countless others who act more like men than most men," a *Village Voice* writer stated. "The tight levis, rough plaid shirt, leather jacket—these are equally the badge of the new American homosexual and of those members of the male alliance trying so desperately to prove their masculinity."

Similarly, Donald Webster Cory and John LeRoy noted "a new stereotype emerging on the American homosexual scene: the muscle-man, the weight-lifter, the barbell collector, the body-worshipping physical culturist who haunts the gym as surely as his effeminate counterpart haunts the drags." Cory and LeRoy reported, "One goes into the apartment of a gay couple, and where once there were pastel shades and lavender curtains, today there are barbells to make the chest muscular and the legs strong." They noted the irony of this hypermasculinity growing "side by side with effeminacy, symbolized by the screaming hairdresser, as the two stereotypes of the homosexual. And why not?" they concluded. "Surely it is clear that they are only reverse sides of a single coin!"

The exasperation that sometimes resulted from these extremes was expressed in a letter to the *Mattachine Review* from Mr. R.A.H., a young man in San Francisco. Consistent with homophile standards, he was dutifully suppressing his own effeminacy and bristling at those who did not follow suit:

"By walking down Market Street, you can well see the faggotts swishing away with their—OH—so sophisticated voices, with the least concern or care toward who sees or hears them.

"Make-up, mascara (sometimes), lipstick—the whole works is used by these faggotts. I'm not one to knock the usage of cosmetics, only when used so thick that anyone could scrape it off with a butter knife and still have some to spare. I wear cosmetics myself, but only to cover blemishes and then I am discreet. I used to be one of them, but I have learned my lesson. That is 'recognition by action and speech.'

"Acceptance into heterosexual society is one of the most important 'firsts' for most homophiles, even to the faggott. For the majority of us, it is due to these faggotts who scream with defiance that we are not accepted.

"Is it not high time that those who still have their wits about them begin to do something to clean up this saddening mess? Or are they scared? Scared so much that it is even still difficult for them to stand up and fight for a right that is being denied them, by cleaning up our own homophile society!

"We want to be accepted. There are hundreds and thousands of heterosexuals who want to accept us, but won't, because some of us haven't earned the right for acceptance or even have the intestinal fortitude to fight for what is right, by cleaning our own house.

"Fighting is easy, if it is done properly and I hardly mean by fists, but by enforcing—that faggotts not be allowed into your gathering places unless they conform.

"It is not hard to make some changes in habit. In the long run, life *will* be worth living, and acceptance will be for all."

Hal Call's reply to this agitated young man reflects basic Mattachine principles tempered by his growing resignation to the realities of gay men's natures: "We agree that defiance and 'way out' expression of one's feelings of rejection by a few brings scorn and derision upon the many. Nevertheless we have also observed that rebellion ignored soon falls flat, and most of these 'social rebels' see the folly of their faggotry in time. . . . But here we see another—and possibly greater sickness on the part of society itself. A new horde of swishes seems to sashay onto the scene every generation. If the majority of society changes its attitude and accepts sexuality for what it is, . . . then we won't have to waste time in the impossible task of remodeling every affected and effeminate swish. After all, the 'harm' he causes is more ephemeral than permanent, more an uncomfortable sting than a damage of consequence."

For American homosexuals, one of the most significant developments of the 1950s was coming to understand themselves as an oppressed minority group. "I believe that our situation is very similar in its broader aspects to that of the Negro," Mr. L. in Baltimore wrote to *ONE*. "Society keeps the

Negro in abject squalor and then takes that imposed condition as proof that the Negro is inferior. We will never know what the Negro is really worth until he is given equality of status and opportunity. The same is true of the homosexual, I am convinced."

Mattachine resisted the minority-group idea, urging homophiles to seek toleration through assimilation-minded conformity. But Mr. E.A.B. in Denver rejected this view. "I believe the time has come for homosexuals to demand their civil rights as aggressively as Negroes are demanding theirs," he stated. "We will get no where by pussy-footing our own cause. In their hearts, people respect those who stick up for their rights, even when by non-violent means. . . . The time has come for social enlightenment on this subject kept so long in the dark in our culture. And some people in their lethargy need to be shocked into consciousness."

The editor's reply was classic Mattachine: "We cannot counsel you to use demands or aggressions and only hope you won't come begging on our doorstep if YOUR aggression stirs up retaliative aggressive acts against YOU. Education and enlightenment are the Mattachine Society's goals, but shock techniques are not its way. Problems disappear through evolution; they are only aggravated by revolution."

Concurring in this view was Mr. K. in Atlanta. "A militant homosexual movement is not called for," he wrote to *ONE*. "Political activity is out of the question. Revolution would mean regression. It may be easier to demand acceptance of the group than for each individual to make himself worthy of acceptance, but only the latter course will effect any lasting change in society's attitude. The question is not *what should be* but *what can be*."

Mr. A. in Upper Darby, Pennsylvania, saw the possibilities differently. "The colored people in the face of prejudice have gotten together to form a union . . . and they are defeating their enemies by getting laws passed," he stated. "Why cannot all of the homosexuals do the same thing . . . ? All that it would take would be a few good, strong leaders to approach the Senators and Congressmen in Washington to sponsor such a bill. There is no reason to consider sex a crime, except our narrow-minded upbringing and training."

John Sheldon in California blasted Mattachine's acquiescent mindset: "Well, you've said your pious little piece again and I suppose all the queer-haters approve, but I wonder how the homosexuals feel. You tell us that 'The law as it exists must be respected and obeyed,' but I say that this is nonsense. Prohibition was destroyed by the millions of decent, liberty-loving American drinkers who simply ignored it, and the present vicious sex laws will eventually be destroyed by the millions of decent, liberty-loving American homosexuals who refuse to have their private lives dictated by a bigoted public. Thoreau wrote on the necessity for civil disobedience. Emerson wrote that anyone trying to enforce the fugitive slave laws should have his head split open with an ax. All through American history there has been the insistence that the individual is superior to the state and that he has the right and duty to resist injustice. We have the right and duty to express our love as we see fit, and I for one intend to fulfill this duty to the best of my ability. The Mattachine Society cannot advocate violation of the law, but you do not have to stoop to such hypocritical humbug as the statement quoted above."

Mr. V.S. in British Columbia deplored the "timid, defensive, apologetic" tone of the *Mattachine Review*: "This business of proclaiming from the housetops that proper queer people are not neurotic, but rather as averagely apple pie-ish and more normal than the 'normals' positively sticks in my craw. Hell, I'm frankly ravingly neurotic and determined to remain that way. I work among 'normals' and have relatives that way and not for anything would I like to be like them or be induced in the slightest to try fitting myself into their social milieu."

So began an era in which the sensibilities of cautious homophiles would be superseded by those of a younger generation that was beginning to talk about gay pride. "After reading ONE I always feel glad, and even proud, that I am homosexual," a college student wrote from Philadelphia. "I am 23 years old and I am Gay," Mr. D. in Ogden, Utah, wrote. "Of this fact I am very proud, as I am sure many others are also."

In 1959 Mr. M. in West Virginia complimented the editor of *ONE* on a change in the magazine's tone: "In 1954 you seemed to say, 'We have these unhappy misfits in our midst—we must do what we can to rehabilitate them.' Now, you seem to say, 'Here we are—all in the same boat. Life and love can still be beautiful, if we will accept ourselves and the courage to be ourselves.' I am very happy over this admirable advance."

Mr. M. in Chicago dreamed big in his letter to *ONE*: "Let's join hands and become a majority and: Transform our individual weaknesses into a tower of united strength, our lonely lives into days full of companionship and joy; live and work for other homosexuals instead of just ourselves . . . ; emphasize the beauty and the good in homosexuality in place of the ugly and evil; help change the laws so we can be law-abiding instead of lawless; help make ONE and other homosexual magazines worthy of their destinies. If we all join hands we can discover a life that is truly Gay! I hope all this does not sound too much like a sermon. In any case, I enclose a small amount for the collection box this Sunday morning."

A benediction of sorts was provided by Mr. R.J. in Oregon: "Let us protect ourselves, do what we can to better ourselves, and accept ourselves better. Above all, let's forget religion, the public, the 'morality' of the times, and the phony institutions that plague us all."

Afterword

AN ILLUMINATING PERIOD PIECE, *Gay Bar* is a small time capsule. Years later we open it and examine the contents, sometimes puzzling over their meaning and significance. Some things we understand well, others not so well. Hard as we may try, we can never fully grasp what life was like for homosexuals in that age of anxiety. American culture has changed so much since then; even the memories of those who remember that period are often unreliable.

Having immersed myself in exploring the circumstances of homosexuals in America in the 1950s, I consider myself lucky to have been born toward the end of that decade. By the time I reached adolescence, American hyperconformity was losing steam. The women's movement, the black civil rights movement, and hippie counterculture were in full swing. The authority of white, heterosexual males was being eroded. Gay men and lesbians were making gains in becoming visible and living authentically.

The origins of America's gay rights movement are usually traced to New York City's Stonewall Inn, when a routine police raid in the summer of 1969 was met with violent resistance. The defiance and self-assertion exhibited by Stonewall patrons had developed gradually through two decades. This transformation in how American homosexuals saw themselves and their place in society began in the 1950s, with the founding of the Mattachine Society and ONE, Incorporated, in Los Angeles, and the Daughters of Bilitis in San Francisco. These organizations fostered the emergence of homosexuals throughout the country, from furtive isolation into a nascent gay community with a minority-group identity.

I am enormously grateful for the pioneering men and women, one and two generations older than I, who came together in the 1950s and launched what would become America's gay rights movement. And I have special appreciation for their allies, those few steadfast "normals" who not only deplored antihomosexualism but stood against it publicly. High-visibility straight allies are not especially numerous today. From that per-spective, Helen Branson's and Blanche Baker's bold initiatives were even more extraordinary.

An article appeared in the *Mattachine Review* shortly after *Gay Bar* was published, in the interest of promoting the book. It was highlighted on the cover of the February 1958 issue: "Helen P. Branson Tells Reasons Why Homosexuals Don't Get Married."

Helen's essay, "Homosexuals—as I See Them," revisits some of her *Gay Bar* observations and includes some noteworthy new material. Of particu-lar interest is Helen's view of the real problem with homosexuality: so many homosexual men not getting married leaves so many heterosexual women high and dry. This analysis may seem rather odd today but it made sense at the time. Historically, most homosexuals had complied with mar-riage expectations. But during the 1950s in Los Angeles, Helen noticed that gay men were increasingly opting out of heterosexual marriage.

In her effort to explain this trend away from marriage, some of Helen's conclusions may be puzzling. In particular, was the inadequacy of women's housekeeping really such a marriage-breaker for gay men? Helen may have been a bit off in her analysis. But it's also possible that we are simply unable to truly grasp the circumstances of the gay men she tells us about, and how those realities shaped their behavior. Imagine homosexual men with the typical gay male mix of domestic, aesthetic, and perfectionistic sensibilities living in that highly conformist climate. Feeling trapped in ill-conceived marriages, seeing no viable alternatives, it's not much of a stretch to imagine that they might fixate on their wives' housekeeping deficiencies, real or imagined. Tranquilizers, anyone?

Perhaps most significant in this essay is Helen's assertion that homosexuality is based less on "sex urges" than on characteristic patterns of the mind and attitudes toward life. This statement is consistent with her remarks in *Gay Bar* about common traits among her boys, but here she goes further: "The sexual aspect is only a minor thing." These are the reflections of a woman who came to know, appreciate, and celebrate gay men over a period of twenty years. In some ways, this palm-reading bartender understood gay men more deeply than many of them understood themselves.

"Homosexuals—as I See Them"

Helen P. Branson's view of homosexuals comes, as she plainly tells, only from her observation of many of them as customers and friends of a bar which she operates. The story of her "Gay Bar" was told in a recent small book by her (reviewed elsewhere in this issue of Mattachine Review*).*

The following article might well be entitled "Reasons Why Homosexuals Don't Get Married," for that is what it is about. Readers of the article, as well as sociologists and psychologists, may disagree with Helen's views, but they can hardly deny that her points have been scored at one time or another by people they know. They may say she has dealt with surface symptoms and not touched all-important root causes—if there are such underlying factors to get at. At any rate Helen's viewpoints are food for thought. Read and see. Then don't be afraid to write if she's wrong.

Everyone has his special reason for making statements about any given subject. This is his point of view, and although he may not agree with others, he has his right to his opinion. I see homosexuality from one viewpoint that many others have not had the opportunity of utilizing.

147

I own and operate a homosexual bar, known as a 'gay' bar. I welcome male homosexuals only. I am in my sixth year of operation and feel that I am in a position to express convictions.

Homosexuality *IS* a problem. It is a deeper one than just unusual sex habits. It is a growing one as these ranks—or knowledge about them—increase. In my opinion, the generally accepted interpretation is a fallacy. By this, I mean the suspicion that homosexuals live for the pleasure of the seduction of teenage boys. This fear has been based on the occasional acts of this nature, but we cannot assume that all heterosexual men seduce young girls just because there is a crime of this nature committed now and then. Any group of people has its few who give the whole clan an unsavory reputation. Most of the homosexuals abhor the exception who is drawn to youths and feel that judges should 'throw the book' at anyone guilty of such practices.

The problem is that such an unbelievably high percentage of adult males are not married and don't intend to be married. This leaves an equally high percentage of females unloved and unmarried.

There are several reasons why the homosexual does not want to marry. The first reason I am giving seems trivial, but I am seeing one 'mixed' marriage break up because of this. It is simply that most women do not keep house well enough for the gay man. I consider myself a neat housekeeper but my house would not suit many of my customers. Their houses or apartments are often decorator's dreams. This mixed marriage that is on the rocks is being wrecked by her slovenly ways in the house after he comes home from work. He has been drinking to forget it and she drinks to keep up with him.

Several years ago the fellow concerned talked to me and his big complaint was her untidiness. This seems exaggerated but nice surroundings are highly important to these boys.

The second of my reasons is that the homosexual does not want to extend himself emotionally for fear of being hurt. Idealism and sensitivity are two very pronounced characteristics of the invert. I see this extreme idealism in my boys all the time. I have in mind one who has gone off the deep end several times since I have been acquainted with him. He talks to me about the new friend who has the same tastes that he has. They both like opera and curry and bicycling and swimming at night. But after they have moved in together, everyday living with its small irritations is too much and there is another move.

There is a third reason in this list. It is the dislike of assuming responsibilities. Many of my boys have had too much responsibility too early and after being set free of this they refuse to accept another liability.

I'm thinking of Larry, whose father was so interested in ward politics that his wife and later Larry, at 15, worked to keep the household (including two other children) in food and clothing. At 16, Larry was earning more than his father. Later when Larry's mother passed on, he moved away and started acquiring some of the nice things he had longed for earlier. He is established now, but his extra time and money are going into a college education. He draws back from the emotional trap of marriage.

The fourth and most powerful reason for not marrying is the divorce laws. These fellows feel that the cards are stacked against them. Regardless of whether the girl knows beforehand or if she discovers the homosexual trait after marriage, the result is generally the same. She can use this as a lever when she demands alimony. He is in a cleft stick. Pay up or be exposed in court and lose his job. Even if he is in business for himself, he does not dare risk the publicity.

In the past year I have been watching a most tragic story unfold. Dave is a quiet, lovable young man who went to high school and has kept in touch with part of his high school gang. He has brought in two or three of this group, none of whom were homosexual. They were aware of this side of his life but loved him for himself. A girl from the former high school group set her cap for Dave. It was quite apparent to me. There was never any discussion about his homosexual side, but she was aware of it as shown by an occasional statement. They were married and Dave was honor bright in his attempt to make this marriage successful. He is very fond of children and they agreed that she would work until a possible pregnancy. They made no effort to prevent this happening and in a few weeks he informed me that he was to be a father and his face was aglow with unmistakable pride.

149

Dave and his wife had bought new furniture for an apartment, going in debt for it. Within three months, in fact as soon as she was positive that she was to have a child, she told him she didn't want to be married. She gave no reason. She had no complaints about his conduct. She just went into the bedroom after dinner, laid on the bed and read. Dave figured that it was a quirk of pregnancy. He was as kind and thoughtful as he could be.

She kept stating that she did not want to be married, that she wanted a divorce. Her parents argued with her, but she was adamant. She went to a lawyer and got a divorce in her fifth or sixth month of pregnancy. She never actually used the homosexual side of his life as a threat, but the thought hovered there. As she got nearer to her time, she quit work. There was a legal agreement about costs of confinement and the period after the baby's birth.

She is working now, her mother cares for the baby and Dave gets to see the little one once a week and take pictures of her, which he brings in for me to see.

When the rift first appeared, I was convinced that her actions could be caused by nutritional deficiencies, but as the case advanced it was obvious to me that hers was a deliberate program. Here was a way to have a legitimate child and be certain there would be no fight when she made the break. She moved 25 miles away, making his weekly visit a hardship of Sunday driving. This action of hers not only spoiled this marriage but it will successfully prevent many others from trying to establish a heterosexual home.

Homosexuality, from my viewpoint, is not primarily based on sex urges. There is a meeting of the minds and an attitude toward life that I do not see in heterosexual life. Possibly the homosexual's hesitance in assuming family life is the basis of the light, airy mannerisms that show so plainly. The quick wit, the saber thrusts at the weak points in another's armor, the spontaneous ingenuity in creating art and beauty are traits prevalent in this group. The sexual aspect is only a minor thing. When the invert lives this life over a period of years and if he is disappointed in his ideals, the sex urge becomes more and more powerful. I know of many older couples who have spent years together. Their lives are united through companionship and love of home.

It is true that some of these men who have lost their companion are now out searching for transitory pleasures. I cannot see any difference [between this and] the actions of a free heterosexual who is hunting brief delights from women.

I do not condone the actions of many young homosexuals who are experimenting in sex procedures but we are blinded by numbers here, not percentages.

Heterosexuals do not know and cannot believe that there is such a huge army of homosexuals. When they see the many obvious deviates, the limp-wristed, hip-swaying exhibitionists, they think they are able to identify members of this group. The truth is that the vast majority of serious homosexuals are as tolerant of these show-offs as are the heterosexuals. Most homosexuals are undetectable to the average person.

They dress conservatively, they hold good jobs and date girls for shows and dancing. Possibly their neatness and good manners would be a clue to the knowing one, but that is all.

They are well-adjusted to their way of life. For an economic reason they conceal this side of living because of the prevalent intolerance, but they have no intention of changing. I hear an occasional "I may get married someday" but that day seldom comes. The small percentage who go to a psychiatrist for an attempted change have their counterpart in the heterosexual who goes for marital troubles or nerves.

I have suggested a psychiatrist occasionally but only because I hoped the boy would learn to live with himself peacefully. I am convinced it is a rare case that can make the change from homosexuality to heterosexuality. Let us accept these gentle, sensitive people as they are and enjoy their talents and their company. We all have habits that could offend someone. Let us look to our own weaknesses first. We might not then have time to censure the other fellow.

Acknowledgments

I AM GRATEFUL TO THE VARIOUS INDIVIDUALS who have helped me in the making of this book.

For many years, Raphael Kadushin and his colleagues at the University of Wisconsin Press have nurtured and brought forth books that document and illuminate queer lives.

Dean Gray's desire to bring *Gay Bar* to life on the stage motivated me to do the research that led to this book.

Kim Karcher's encouraging advice helped me to find Helen Branson's descendants.

Caroline Branson Hammond and Russell Hammond were splendid informants, helping me to gain a better understanding of Helen Branson.

Conversations with Diane Been, Deborah Conta, and Finbar Maxwell helped to develop and clarify my understanding of Helen and her world.

Loni Shibuyama at the ONE National Gay and Lesbian Archives was wonderfully helpful in supplying various documents, as was Rebekah Kim at the GLBT Historical Society.

Max Yela, Michael Doylen, and their colleagues at the University of Wisconsin–Milwaukee Libraries assisted my immersion in 1950s homophile publications and ephemera.

Carson Anderson, Jay Jones, and Gerry Takano assisted my exploration of 1950s gay L.A.

Bronze Quinton—my life partner, steadfast supporter, and crucial critic—enabled me to find the time and solitude necessary for this work.

I dedicate this revival of *Gay Bar* to the memory of those who resisted the tyranny of midcentury conformism and to the memory of those who did not make it through.

Notes on Sources

Book epigraph

vi   "In the millions who are silent . . ." is from Donald Webster Cory, *The Homosexual in America: A Subjective Approach* (New York: Greenberg, 1951), 91.

Preface

x   "So long as 'omniscient' psychiatry . . ." is from *Mattachine Review*, November–December 1955, 27.

xi   "the creeping scourge of mediocrity . . ." is from *Mattachine Review*, August 1957, 15.

xi   "In our culture, the spiritless homosexual . . ." is from *Mattachine Review*, April 1958, 32.

xii   "all pretended to be more effeminate . . ." is from *ONE*, April 1961, 30.

xii   "Many of today's gays . . ." is from Donald Vining, *How Can You Come Out If You've Never Been In?* (Trumansburg, N.Y.: Crossing, 1986), 53–54.

xii   Albert Ellis's advice to homosexuals is from J. D. Mercer, *They Walk in Shadow* (New York: Comet, 1959), 474–75.

xiii   "bitchery-butchery," "One of our headaches . . . ," and "for only the holiest of holies . . ." are from James T. Sears, *Behind the Mask of the Mattachine: The Hal Call Chronicles and the Early Movement for Homosexual Emancipation* (Binghamton, N.Y.: Harrington Park, 2006), 398, 405, 307.

xiv "People still think in terms . . ." is from Donald Webster Cory and John P. LeRoy, *The Homosexual and His Society: A View from Within* (New York: Citadel, 1963), 4.

Commentary Following Text from Dust Jacket of Original Edition

xviii Caroline Branson Hammond quotes are from my conversations with her, October 2008 to January 2009. Other details about Helen Branson's life are from those conversations and from conversations with Albert Russell Hammond, Helen's grandson, October 2008 to July 2009.

Commentary Following Introduction by Blanche M. Baker, M.D.

11 Many details concerning the original publication of *Gay Bar* are from the Harold L. Call Papers, ONE National Gay and Lesbian Archives, Los Angeles.

11 "Jehovah's Witnesses would ring . . ." is from my conversation with Helen Branson's grandson, Russ Hammond.

11 "My stress is on self-acceptance . . ." is from *ONE*, January 1959, 26–27.

12 Stekel quotes are from Wilhelm Stekel, *The Homosexual Neurosis* (New York: Emerson, 1946), 286, 306, 309, 313–14.

12 Bergler quotes are from Edmund Bergler, *Homosexuality: Disease or Way of Life?* (New York: Hill and Wang, 1957), 9, 28.

12 "While I do not belong . . ." is from *ONE*, September 1959, 28.

13 The story of "one man's psychoanalytic odyssey" is from Will Fellows, *Farm Boys: Lives of Gay Men from the Rural Midwest* (Madison: University of Wisconsin Press, 1996), 42–44.

13 "a practicing homosexual with no . . ." is from Isadore Rubin, ed., *The "Third Sex"* (New York: New Book, 1961), 76.

13 "a particularly difficult case . . ." is from Charles Berg and Clifford Allen, *The Problem of Homosexuality* (New York: Citadel, 1958), 83–84.

14 "Homosexuality can be the result . . ." is from Gina Cerminara, *The World Within* (New York: Sloane, 1957), 112.

14 "the transition period of leaving . . ." is from *ONE*, November 1959, 30.

14 "A figure-eight lower loop . . ." is from *The Ladder*, October 1957, 18–20.

14 "Dr. B. is guilty of identifying . . ." is from *The Ladder*, April 1957, 5–6.

15 "a biological anomaly . . ." is from Gordon Westwood, *A Minority* (London: Longmans, 1960), 17.

16 "Many creative fields lie ahead . . ." is from *The Ladder*, May 1957, 6.

16 "Since the mother is the first . . . ," "in a bewildering pattern . . . ," and "when hostile attitudes . . ." are from *ONE*, July 1959, 26–27.

17 "a straight line ranging . . ." and "the infinitely varied sexual makeup . . ." are from Gavin Arthur, *The Circle of Sex* (San Francisco: Pan-Graphic, 1962), page 13 and dust jacket.

17 "shows many of the characteristics . . ." is from *ONE*, October 1959, 27.

17 "that much of the alcoholism . . ." and "the almost feverish demand . . ." are from Gavin Arthur, *Circle of Sex*, 11, 85.

18 "We are coming into a period . . ." is from "The Homosexual in Our Society," a radio panel discussion recorded May 2, 1958, and broadcast November 24, 1958, by KPFA-FM, San Francisco. Moderated by KPFA staffer Elsa Knight Thompson, the panel included Blanche Baker, psychiatrist; Hal Call, *Mattachine Review* editor; and Leah Gailey, mother of a gay son. The program was broadcast in Los Angeles and New York in 1959. Pacifica Radio Archives supplied a recording. Transcript is in *Mattachine Review*, July 1960, 12–28.

18 "Within the topmost glitter . . ." is from *ONE*, April 1960, 31.

18 "Please tell me . . ." is from *ONE*, June 1960, 28.

18 "With the coming of spring . . ." and Blanche's reply are from *ONE*, April 1960, 27.

19 "I am convinced . . ." is from *ONE*, October 1959, 28–29.

Commentary Following Foreword and Chapter 1

29 "non-conformism is the major . . ." is from Robert Lindner, *Must You Conform?* (New York: Rinehart, 1955), 33.

29 "upholders of the official morality . . ." is from Cory and LeRoy, *Homosexual and His Society*, 74.

29 "politically and propagandistically . . ." is from A. M. Krich, ed., *The Homosexuals—As Seen by Themselves and Thirty Authorities* (New York: Citadel, 1954), 248.

30 Newspaper advice column reprint is from *Mattachine Review*, February 1959, 28–29.

30 Minneapolis newspaper column reprint is from *Mattachine Review*, May–June 1955, 24–30.

31 "In the early 1950s . . ." is from John Gerassi, *The Boys of Boise: Furor, Vice, and Folly in an American City* (Seattle: University of Washington Press, 2001), 49.

31 "being on the outskirts . . ." is from Lillian Faderman and Stuart Timmons,

Gay L.A.: A History of Sexual Outlaws, Power Politics, and Lipstick Lesbians (New York: Basic, 2006), 99.

31   "Especially in the larger cities . . ." is from Mercer, *They Walk in Shadow*, 244–45.

32   "Gay bars! . . ." is from Cory, *Homosexual in America*, 121–22.

32   "The atmosphere is generally . . ." is from Cory and LeRoy, *Homosexual and His Society*, 111.

32   "It should come as no surprise . . ." is from Faderman and Timmons, *Gay L.A.*, 146.

33   "In Hollywood you may find . . ." is from Howard Norton, *The Third Sex* (Portland, Ore.: Facts, 1949), 40.

Commentary Following Chapters 2 and 3

45   "My younger brothers were interested . . ." and "When we chose up sides . . ." are from Sears, *Behind the Mask of the Mattachine*, 333, 76–77.

46   "I never wanted to stand . . . ," "sissified," and "wasn't a flamboyant . . ." are from Sears, *Behind the Mask of the Mattachine*, 33, 123, 104.

46   "We accept the fact . . ." and "Part of our excitement . . ." are from Sears, *Behind the Mask of the Mattachine*, 405, 179.

46   "Many homosexuals consider . . ." is from Cory, *Homosexual in America*, 230.

48   "The Margin of Masculinity" quotations are from *ONE*, May 1955, 7–18.

49   "Does he deserve the scorn . . ." is from *Mattachine Review*, October 1958, cover.

49   "Swish or Swim" quotations are from *ONE*, January 1959, 6–9.

49   "Just now American society . . ." is from *Mattachine Review*, May 1959, 12.

49   "While some may argue . . ." is from *ONE*, September 1955, 28.

49   "The flaming faggot who swishes . . ." is from *ONE*, May 1954, 28.

50   "I am a firm believer . . ." is from *ONE*, April 1959, 29.

50   "I . . . was born with my characteristics . . ." is from *ONE*, October 1958, 30.

51   "How helpful it would be . . ." is from *Mattachine Review*, April 1958, 31.

51   "a most unfortunate and ill-advised item . . ." is from *ONE*, September 1955, 26.

51   "The public likes nothing better . . ." is from *ONE*, September 1955, 27.

51   "Most normal people . . ." is from *ONE*, February 1959, 28.

52   "I know that many people . . ." is from *ONE*, March 1960, 32.

52   "I am a man sixty-one . . ." is from *ONE*, October 1958, 29.

53 "A homosexual to 'Mr. Jones' . . ." is from *Mattachine Review*, March 1960, 27.

53 "There is no reason . . ." is from *ONE*, May 1960, 29.

53 "The homosexual contributes so much . . ." is from *ONE*, March 1958, 30.

53 "I don't claim to have . . ." is from *ONE*, October 1958, 29.

53 "Being in the life . . ." is from *ONE*, May 1958, 31.

54 "During my entire adult life . . ." is from *Mattachine Review*, December 1958, 8.

54 "We are the furtive . . ." is from *Mattachine Review*, August 1958, 12–13.

55 Blanche Baker and Hal Call quotes from the 1958 radio panel discussion "The Homosexual in Our Society" are from *Mattachine Review*, July 1960, 12–28.

56 "I do not claim . . ." is from *ONE*, September 1959, 28.

Commentary Following Chapters 4 and 5

72 "Outrageous they may be . . ." is from Cory and LeRoy, *Homosexual and His Society*, 118.

72 "I have on several occasions . . ." is from *ONE*, February 1958, 8.

72 "a Latin organist . . ." is from L. Jay Barrow, *Hollywood . . . Gay Capitol of the World* (Van Nuys, Calif.: Triumph News, 1968), 68.

72 "hustlers, drunkards, vice cops . . ." is from Bill Adair, Moira Kennedy, and Jeffrey B. Samudio, *Gay and Lesbian L.A. History Map* (Hollywood: Los Angeles Gay and Lesbian History Research Project, 2000), note 2.

73 "resort for illegal possessors . . ." is from *ONE*, March 1959, 7.

73 "that a license may not be suspended . . ." is from *Mattachine Review*, February 1959, 25.

74 "Occasionally, but not frequently . . ." is from Cory and LeRoy, *The Homosexual in His Society*, 117.

74 "The police are alarmed . . ." is from *ONE*, October–November 1957, 20.

75 "in one city after another . . ." is from *ONE*, April 1961, 30.

75 "Vice cops were to be found . . ." is from Lester Strong and David Hanna, "Hollywood Watering Holes, 30s Style," *Harvard Gay and Lesbian Review* 3 (Summer 1996): 30–33.

75 "They were assassinating character . . ." is from Eric Marcus, *Making History: The Struggle for Gay and Lesbian Equal Rights, 1945–1990, An Oral History* (New York: HarperCollins, 1992), 63.

75 "Going to gay bars . . ." and "Will this be the night . . ." are from Sears, *Behind the Mask of the Mattachine*, 161.

75 "One is not surprised . . ." is from *ONE*, February 1958, 7.

76 "Improper touching," "Offer to provide sexual services," and "Solicitation of sexual services" are from Faderman and Timmons, *Gay L.A.*, 86.

76 Dale Jennings's arrest and trial details are from Sears, *Behind the Mask of the Mattachine*, 163–64.

77 "The cops could do any damn thing . . ." is from Marcus, *Making History*, 63–64.

77 "It was too dangerous . . ." is from Sears, *Behind the Mask of the Mattachine*, 21–22.

77 "The male homosexual . . ." is from Marcus, *Making History*, 61–62.

77 "The boys are so horny . . ." is from Faderman and Timmons, *Gay L.A.*, 127.

77 "a lot of animosity . . ." is from Marcus, *Making History*, 77.

77 "are people like other people" is from Sears, *Behind the Mask of the Mattachine*, 207.

78 "As much as I'm ashamed . . ." is from *Mattachine Review*, November 1960, 28.

78 "Why should I join . . ." is from *Mattachine Review*, June 1956, 32.

78 "Homosexuals, as a group . . ." and "If a pamphlet for the initiated . . ." are from Sears, *Behind the Mask of the Mattachine*, 437, 97.

Commentary Following Chapter 6

83 "Among homosexuals the feeling . . ." is from *ONE*, February 1958, 7.

83 "There is much persecution . . ." is from *ONE*, February 1959, 28.

83 "Seeing your outstanding example . . ." is from *ONE*, June–July 1956, 46.

83 "If anyone would know . . ." is from *ONE*, March 1959, 26.

83 "I have taken interest . . ." is from *Mattachine Review*, February 1957, 29.

84 "I am 26, very lonely . . ." is from *ONE*, January 1958, 30.

84 "I'm in my early twenties . . ." is from *ONE*, March 1958, 29.

85 B.C.'s letter and Blanche's reply are from *ONE*, June 1959, 26–28.

86 J.H.D.'s letter is from *ONE*, September 1959, 26–27.

87 "I am a very happy . . ." is from *ONE*, February 1960, 31.

87 "I am no youngster . . ." is from *ONE*, September 1960, 31.

88 C.L.R.'s letter and Blanche's reply are from *ONE*, December 1959, 23–26.

Commentary Following Chapters 7 and 8

102 Caroline Branson Hammond quotations are from my conversations with her, October 2008 to January 2009. Other details about Helen Branson's

life are from those conversations and from conversations with Albert Russell Hammond, Helen's grandson, October 2008 to July 2009.

102 "Speak honestly, truthfully . . ." is from Cheiro (Count Louis Hamon), *Cheiro's Language of the Hand* (1894; repr. Alexandria, Va.: Time-Life, 1992), 161.

103 Astrologer's "psychological problems" ad is from *ONE*, September 1953, 24.

103 "I am not one of your subscribers . . ." is from *ONE*, September 1955, 28.

103 "The homosexuals require a closer . . ." is from *ONE*, April 1958, 29.

103 "The answer to the riddle . . ." is from *ONE*, December 1957, 30.

104 "Now keep this to yourself . . ." and "He really loved his mother . . ." are from Sears, *Behind the Mask of the Mattachine*, 136–37, 510.

104 "Just between Us Mothers" is from *Mattachine Review*, June 1957, 20–22.

107 Fort Worth newspaper article reprint is from *Mattachine Review*, April 1958, 12–13.

108 "Your attack on Dr. Bergler . . ." is from *ONE*, May 1960, 30.

108 "I am not of the Gay World . . ." is from *ONE*, August 1958, 29.

109 "I have a grandson . . ." is from *ONE*, April 1959, 31.

109 Leah Gailey article is from *Mattachine Review*, May 1958, 5–8.

110 "I had promised the gay men . . ." is from Marcus, *Making History*, 25.

Commentary Following Chapters 9 and 10

121 Mattachini Players production notice is from *The Ladder*, April 1957, 7.

121 "*They never fight back* . . ." is from Cory, *Homosexual in America*, 39.

121 "Until the colored people . . ." is from *ONE*, May 1959, 29.

121 "Homosexuals *as a group* . . ." is from *Mattachine Review*, May 1959, 8.

122 "Yes, I am as much of a variant . . ." is from *Mattachine Review*, June 1959, 29.

122 "Lying and hypocrisy . . ." is from *Mattachine Review*, April 1956, 34–36.

123 "Let's face it, fellows . . ." is from *ONE*, June 1953, 20.

123 "Lately I've read ONE . . ." is from *ONE*, December 1955, 29.

123 "That your motives . . ." is from *ONE*, October 1958, 30.

124 "(1) that homosexuality is incurable . . ." is from Rubin, *"Third Sex,"* 69.

124 "causes of homosexualism . . ." and "The psychiatrists . . . will tell the invert . . ." are from Cory, *Homosexual in America*, 72 184.

125 "I always tell them . . ." is from the transcript of the 1958 radio panel discussion "The Homosexual in Our Society," *Mattachine Review*, July 1960, 12–28.

126 "How foolish! . . ." is from *Mattachine Review*, April 1959, 19.

126 "Our society is preoccupied . . ." is from Cory and LeRoy, *Homosexual and His Society*, 229.

126 "God! Mother was unrelenting . . ." is from Sears, *Behind the Mask of the Mattachine*, 31.

126 "Is marriage the answer . . ." is from Cory, *Homosexual in America*, 200.

126 "Recently I met . . ." and Blanche's reply are from *ONE*, February 1959, 26.

127 "It would seem from my . . ." is from Cory, *Homosexual in America*, 201.

127 "many homosexuals tend to sentimentalize . . ." is from *Mattachine Review*, July–August 1955, 10.

127 "'All you need is a woman!' . . . ," "It is true that many . . . ," and "how many of these . . ." are from Cory, *Homosexual in America*, 261, 183, 205.

128 "may marry, have children . . ." is from Mercer, *They Walk in Shadow*, 517.

128 "sex-love involvements . . ." is from Rubin, *"Third Sex,"* 57.

128 "I say Dr. Albert Ellis . . ." is from *ONE*, November 1960, 30.

128 "If you think homosexuals . . ." is from *ONE*, December 1957, 5.

Commentary Following "For the Record"

132 "we would not consider . . ." is from a February 1957 letter to Harold Sylvester, Brunswick, Ohio, Donald S. Lucas Papers, GLBT Historical Society, San Francisco.

132 Exchanges between Helen Branson and Hal Call are from Call Papers, ONE National Gay and Lesbian Archives, Los Angeles.

132 "mother hen guarding . . ." is from Sears, *Behind the Mask of the Mattachine*, 370.

133 *ONE*'s review of *Gay Bar* is from January 1958, 22.

133 *Mattachine Review*'s review of *Gay Bar* is from February 1958, 20–22.

134 *The Ladder*'s review of *Gay Bar* is from February 1958, 14.

134 "providing a great discussion provoker . . ." is from *ONE*, March 1958, 30.

134 "I cannot recall reading a duller . . ." is from *ONE*, February 1958, 31.

135 "It was not like a story . . ." is from *Mattachine Review*, March 1958, 31.

135 "I'm a true female . . ." and Blanche's reply are from *ONE*, June 1960, 29.

136 Details on Helen's life after leaving Los Angeles are from conversations with her daughter and grandson.

137 "It is an undeniable . . ." is from *Mattachine Review*, August 1956, 8.

137 "A sociologist writing . . ." is from Cory, *Homosexual in America*, 227–28.

138 "'Homosexual problem,' etc. . . ." is from *ONE*, March 1959, 29.

138 "every device human ingenuity . . ." is from *ONE*, December 1957, 5.

138   "Their need for hatred . . ." is from Cory, *Homosexual in America*, 263.

138   "You must take the realistic view . . ." is from Gerassi, *Boys of Boise*, 62.

138   Observation from Bowman speech is from *The Ladder*, March 1959, 4.

138   "Depth study . . ." is from Cory and LeRoy, *Homosexual and His Society*, 256.

139   *Village Voice* article reprint is from *Mattachine Review*, May 1959, 10.

139   "a new stereotype emerging . . . ," "one goes into the apartment . . . ," and "side by side with effeminacy . . ." are from Cory and LeRoy, *Homosexual and His Society*, 4, 83, 91.

139   "By walking down Market Street . . ." and Hal Call's reply are from *Mattachine Review*, December 1962, 34–35.

140   "I believe that our situation . . ." is from *ONE*, June–July 1957, 31.

141   "I believe the time has come . . ." and the editor's reply are from *Mattachine Review*, October 1957, 35.

141   "A militant homosexual movement . . ." is from *ONE*, January 1958, 31.

141   "The colored people . . ." is from *ONE*, May 1959, 29.

142   "Well, you've said your pious . . ." is from *Mattachine Review*, July 1960, 32.

142   "timid, defensive, apologetic" is from *Mattachine Review*, October 1960, 23.

142   "After reading ONE . . ." and "I am 23 years old . . ." are from *ONE*, June 1959, 29–30.

142   "In 1954 you seemed to say . . ." is from *ONE*, December 1959, 29–30.

143   "Let's join hands . . ." is from *ONE*, October 1959, 30.

143   "Let us protect ourselves . . ." is from *Mattachine Review*, December 1958, 26.

Bibliography

THE FOLLOWING BOOKS have informed my understanding of the circumstances of homosexuals in America in the 1950s.

Adam, Barry D. *The Rise of a Gay and Lesbian Movement*. Boston: Twayne, 1987.

Arthur, Gavin. *The Circle of Sex*. San Francisco: Pan-Graphic, 1962.

Berg, Charles, and Clifford Allen. *The Problem of Homosexuality*. New York: Citadel, 1958.

Bergler, Edmund. *Homosexuality: Disease or Way of Life?* New York: Hill and Wang, 1957.

Cory, Donald Webster. *The Homosexual in America: A Subjective Approach*. New York: Greenberg, 1951.

———, and John P. LeRoy. *The Homosexual and His Society: A View from Within*. New York: Citadel, 1963.

D'Emilio, John. *Sexual Politics, Sexual Communities: The Making of a Homosexual Minority in the United States, 1949–1970*. Chicago: University of Chicago Press, 1983.

Faderman, Lillian, and Stuart Timmons. *Gay L.A.: A History of Sexual Outlaws, Power Politics, and Lipstick Lesbians*. New York: Basic, 2006.

Gerassi, John. *The Boys of Boise: Furor, Vice, and Folly in an American City*. Seattle: University of Washington Press, 2001.

Krich, A. M., ed. *The Homosexuals—As Seen by Themselves and Thirty Authorities*. New York: Citadel, 1954.

Lindner, Robert. *Must You Conform?* New York: Rinehart, 1955.

Loughery, John. *The Other Side of Silence: Men's Lives and Gay Identities: A Twentieth-Century History*. New York: Henry Holt, 1998.

Marcus, Eric. *Making History: The Struggle for Gay and Lesbian Equal Rights, 1945–1990, An Oral History*. New York: HarperCollins, 1992.

Mercer, J. D. *They Walk in Shadow*. New York: Comet, 1959.

Miller, Neil. *Sex-Crime Panic: A Journey to the Paranoid Heart of the 1950s*. Los Angeles: Alyson, 2002.

Nardi, Peter M., David Sanders, and Judd Marmor. *Growing Up before Stonewall: Life Stories of Some Gay Men*. New York: Routledge, 1994.

Norton, Howard. *The Third Sex*. Portland, Oregon: Facts, 1949.

Rubin, Isadore, ed. *The "Third Sex."* New York: New Book, 1961.

Sears, James T. *Behind the Mask of the Mattachine: The Hal Call Chronicles and the Early Movement for Homosexual Emancipation*. Binghamton, N.Y.: Harrington Park, 2006.

Stekel, Wilhelm. *The Homosexual Neurosis*. New York: Emerson, 1946.

Vacha, Keith. *Quiet Fire: Memoirs of Older Gay Men*. Trumansburg, N.Y.: Crossing, 1985.

Vining, Donald. *How Can You Come Out If You've Never Been In?* Trumansburg, N.Y.: Crossing, 1986.

White, C. Todd. *Pre-Gay L.A.: A Social History of the Movement for Homosexual Rights*. Urbana: University of Illinois Press, 2009.